BILLY GRAHAM
Evangelistic Association
Always Good News.

Dear Friend,

I am pleased to send you this copy of the classic book *In His Steps* by Charles M. Sheldon. I pray you'll be inspired by his compelling story of Christians who dared to ask the important question: "What would Jesus do?"

Following in the footsteps of Jesus can be hard, as this book illustrates. Deciding to act in obedience to the Holy Spirit, rather than simply following along with the world, can sometimes cause conflict, misunderstanding, and rejection. But if we choose to *"not walk according to the flesh but according to the Spirit"* (Romans 8:4, NKJV), we will always enjoy His peace and companionship. My prayer is that God will use this book to encourage you to consider Him in all your decisions and, out of your obedience, to help others find new life in Christ.

For 60 years the Billy Graham Evangelistic Association has worked to take the Good News of Jesus Christ throughout the world by every effective means available, and I'm excited about what God will do in the years ahead.

We would appreciate knowing how our ministry has touched your life. May God richly bless you.

Sincerely,

Franklin Graham
President

If you would like to know more about our ministry, please contact us:

In the U.S.:

Billy Graham Evangelistic Association
1 Billy Graham Parkway
Charlotte, NC 28201-0001
billygraham.org
info@bgea.org
Toll-free: 1-877-2GRAHAM (1-877-247-2426)

In Canada:

Billy Graham Evangelistic Association of Canada
20 Hopewell Way NE
Calgary, AB T3J 5H5
billygraham.ca
Toll-free: 1-888-393-0003

In His Steps

Charles M. Sheldon

This *Billy Graham Library Selection* is published by
Billy Graham Evangelistic Association
with permission from Barbour Publishing.

BARBOUR
PUBLISHING

Originally published in 1896

©2010 by Barbour Publishing, Inc.

Previous ISBN 978-1-60260-854-2
ISBN 978-1-59328-276-9

All scripture quotations are taken from the King James Version of the Bible.

Cover image ©Michael Trevillion/Trevillion Images

Published by Barbour Publishing, Inc., P.O. Box 719, Uhrichsville, Ohio 44683, barbourbooks.com

Our mission is to publish and distribute inspirational products offering exceptional value and biblical encouragement to the masses.

 Member of the
Evangelical Christian
Publishers Association

Printed in the United States of America.

Chapter 1

One Friday morning the Reverend Henry Maxwell tried to finish his Sunday morning sermon. Interrupted several times, he grew nervous as the morning wore away.

"Mary," he called to his wife, as he went upstairs after the last interruption, "if anyone comes, I wish you would say I am very busy and cannot come down."

"But I am going over to visit the kindergarten. You will have the house all to yourself."

In a few minutes he heard his wife go out, and everything was quiet. He settled himself at his desk with a sigh of relief. His text was from 1 Peter 2:21: "For even hereunto were ye called: because Christ also suffered for us, leaving us an example, that ye should follow his steps."

In the first part of the sermon he emphasized the atonement as a personal sacrifice, calling attention to the fact of Jesus' suffering in His life as well as in His death. He then went on to emphasize the atonement from Jesus' life and teachings to show how faith in Christ helped to save human beings because of the pattern or character He displayed for their imitation. He was now on the third and last point, the necessity of following Jesus in His sacrifice and example.

He wrote, "Three steps. What are they?" and was about to enumerate them in logical order when the bell rang. Henry Maxwell frowned and made no movement to answer it. When the bell rang again, he rose and walked over to a window that commanded the view of the front door. A very shabbily dressed young man stood on the steps. "Looks like a tramp," said the minister. "I suppose

I'll have to go down and—"

He went downstairs and opened the front door. After a moment's pause the young man said, "I'm out of a job, sir, and thought maybe you might help me."

"I don't know of anything. Jobs are scarce—," replied the minister, beginning to shut the door slowly.

"I thought you might be able to give me a reference to the city railway or the superintendent of the shops or something," continued the young man, shifting his faded hat from one hand to the other.

"It wouldn't help. You will have to excuse me. I am very busy this morning. I hope you find something."

Mr. Maxwell closed the door and heard the man walk down the steps. As he went up into his study, he saw from his hall window that the man moved slowly down the street, still holding his hat between his hands. Something in the figure so dejected, homeless, and forsaken caused the minister to hesitate a moment as he watched. Then he turned to his desk and with a sigh began writing where he had left off.

"A queer thing happened at the kindergarten this morning, Henry," said his wife while they were eating dinner. "Just after the games the door opened and a young man came in holding a dirty hat in both hands. He sat down near the door and never said a word. He was evidently a tramp, and Miss Wren and Miss Kyle were a little frightened at first, but he sat there very quietly, and after a few minutes he went out."

"The same man called here, I think. Did you say he looked like a tramp?"

"Yes, very dusty, shabby, and generally tramplike. Not more than thirty or thirty-three years old, I should say."

"The same man," said the minister thoughtfully.

"Did you finish your sermon, Henry?" his wife asked after a pause.

"Yes, all done. It has been a very busy week, and the two sermons have cost me a good deal of labor."

"They will be appreciated by a large audience Sunday," replied his wife, smiling. "I hope it won't rain Sunday."

Mr. Maxwell sighed as he thought of the careful, laborious effort he had made in preparing sermons for large audiences that failed to appear.

But when Sunday morning dawned on the town of Raymond, the air was clear and bracing, the sky free from all threatening signs. The service opened at eleven o'clock, and the large building was filled with an audience of the best-dressed, most comfortable-looking people of Raymond.

The First Church of Raymond was the first in the city, with a membership composed of the representatives of the wealth, society, and intelligence of Raymond. It believed in having the best music that money could buy, and its choir was a source of great pleasure to the congregation. The anthem was an elaborate adaptation of the words "Jesus, I my cross have taken, all to leave and follow Thee."

Just before the sermon the soprano sang a solo. There was a general rustle of expectation over the audience as Rachel Winslow stood up behind the screen of carved oak, and Mr. Maxwell settled himself contentedly behind the pulpit. Rachel's voice was even more beautiful than her face as she sang, "Where He leads me I will follow; I'll go with Him, with Him, all the way."

Henry Maxwell felt a glow of satisfaction as he rose to speak, and it was reflected in his delivery of the sermon. The pastor of the First Church loved to preach. The half hour he faced a church full of people exhilarated him. The sermon was interesting, spoken with the passion of a dramatic utterance that had the good taste never to offend with a suspicion of ranting or declamation.

The sermon came to a close, and Mr. Maxwell was about to sit down as the quartet rose to sing the closing selection, when a man's voice coming from the rear of the church startled the entire congregation. The next moment a man came out of the shadow there and walked down the middle aisle. Before the stunned congregation realized what was going on, the man reached the open space in front of the pulpit and turned around, facing the people. It was so unexpected that it offered no room for argument or resistance.

"I've been wondering since I came in here," he said, "if it would be okay to say a word at the close of the service. I'm not drunk and I'm not crazy. I am perfectly harmless, but if I die, as there is every likelihood I shall in a few days, I want the satisfaction of thinking that I said my say in a place like this and before this sort of a crowd."

Mr. Maxwell remained standing, leaning on his pulpit, looking down at the stranger. It was the same dusty, worn, shabby-looking young man who had come to his house the Friday before. He still held his faded hat in his two hands. There was nothing offensive in the man's manner or tone. He was not excited, and he spoke in a low but distinct voice.

The stranger went on as if he had no thought of the unusual element that he had introduced into the decorum of the First Church service. "I'm not an ordinary tramp, though I don't know of any teaching of Jesus that makes one kind of a tramp less worth saving than another. Do you?" He put the question as naturally as if the whole congregation had been a small Bible class. He paused just a moment and coughed painfully. "I am a printer by trade. The new linotype machines are beautiful specimens of invention, but I lost my job ten months ago on account of those machines. I never learned but the one trade, and that's all I can do. I've tramped all over the country trying to find work. I'm not complaining, am I? Just stating facts.

"I've tramped through this city for three days trying to find a job; and in all that time I've not had a word of sympathy or comfort except from your minister here, who said he was sorry for me and hoped I would find a job somewhere.

"Of course, I know you can't all go out of your way to hunt up jobs for other people like me. I'm not asking you to; but what I feel puzzled about is what you mean when you sing, 'I'll go with Him, with Him, all the way.' Do you mean that you are suffering and denying yourselves and trying to save lost, suffering humanity just as I understand Jesus did?

"What did He mean when He said, 'Follow me'? The minister said"—the man turned about and looked up at the pulpit—"that it is necessary for the disciple of Jesus to follow His steps, and he said the steps are 'obedience, faith, love, and imitation.' But I did not hear him tell you just what he meant, especially the last step.

"Somehow I get puzzled when I see so many Christians living in luxury and singing, 'Jesus, I my cross have taken, all to leave and follow Thee,' and remember how my wife died in a tenement in New York City four months ago, gasping for air and asking God to take my little girl, too.

"Of course I don't expect you people can prevent everyone from dying of starvation, lack of proper nourishment, and tenement air, but what does following Jesus mean? It seems to me there's an awful lot of trouble in the world that somehow wouldn't exist if all the people who sing such songs as 'All for Jesus, all for Jesus, all my being's ransomed powers; all my thoughts, and all my doing, all my days, and all my hours' went and lived them out.

"What would Jesus do? Is that what you mean by following His steps? It seems to me the people in the big churches have good clothes and nice houses to live in and money to spend for luxuries and summer vacations and all that, while the people outside the churches, thousands of them, die in tenements and walk the streets for jobs and never have a piano or a picture in the house and grow up in misery and drunkenness and sin."

The man suddenly gave a queer lurch over in the direction of the communion table and laid one grimy hand on it. His hat fell upon the carpet at his feet. A stir went through the congregation. Dr. West half rose from his pew, but as yet the silence was unbroken by any voice or movement worth mentioning in the audience. The man passed his other hand across his eyes and then, without any warning, fell heavily forward on his face, full length up the aisle.

Henry Maxwell spoke: "We will consider the service closed."

He was down the pulpit stairs and kneeling by the prostrate form before anyone else.

Chapter 2

The man lay on the couch in the pastor's study and breathed heavily. When the question of what to do with him came up, the minister insisted on taking charge of the man, and with the entrance of that humanity into the minister's spare room, a new chapter in Henry Maxwell's life began.

The third day after the stranger entered the minister's house, there was a marked change in his condition. But Sunday morning, just before the clock struck one, he rallied and spoke with great difficulty. "You have been good to me. Somehow I feel as if it was what Jesus would do."

After a few minutes he turned his head slightly, and before Mr. Maxwell could realize the fact, the doctor said quietly, "He is gone."

That Sunday morning Mr. Maxwell entered his pulpit to face one of the largest congregations that had ever crowded the First Church. He was haggard and looked as if he had just risen from a long illness. His sermon this morning was neither striking nor impressive. He talked with considerable hesitation. It was evident that some great idea struggled in his thought for utterance, but it was not expressed in the theme he had chosen. Near the close of his sermon, he gathered a certain strength that had been painfully lacking at the beginning.

He closed the Bible, stepped to the side of the pulpit, and faced his people.

"Our brother passed away this morning. I have not yet had time to learn all his history. He had one sister living in Chicago. I have written her and have not yet received an answer."

He paused and looked over the house. He had never seen so

many earnest faces during his entire pastorate. He was not able yet to tell his people his experiences, the crisis through which he was even now moving. But he didn't feel it was careless impulse that caused him to tell them something of the message he bore in his heart.

So he went on. "The stranger's appearance and words in church last Sunday made a very powerful impression on me. I am not able to conceal from you or myself the fact that what he said has compelled me to ask as I never asked before, 'What does following Jesus mean?' A good deal that was said here last Sunday was in the nature of a challenge to Christianity as it is seen and felt in our churches. And I do not know that any time is more appropriate than the present for me to propose a plan which has been forming in my mind as a satisfactory reply."

Again Henry Maxwell paused and looked into the faces of his people. There were some strong, earnest men and women in the First Church.

He saw Edward Norman, editor of the Raymond *Daily News*, who had been a member of the First Church for ten years. Alexander Powers was superintendent of the great railroad shops in Raymond. There sat Donald Marsh, president of Lincoln College, located in the suburbs of Raymond. Milton Wright, one of the great merchants of Raymond, had in his employ at least one hundred men in various shops. Dr. West, still comparatively young, was quoted as authority in special surgical cases. Young Jasper Chase, the author, had written one successful book and was said to be at work on a new novel. Miss Virginia Page had inherited at least a million dollars through the recent death of her father. And not least of all, Rachel Winslow, from her seat in the choir, glowed with her peculiar beauty of light.

"What I am going to propose now is something which ought not to appear unusual or at all impossible of execution. I want volunteers from the First Church who will pledge themselves, earnestly and honestly for an entire year, not to do anything without first asking the question, 'What would Jesus do?'

"At the close of the service, all those members who are willing to join such a group may stay, and we will talk over the details of the plan. I will of course include myself in this company of volunteers. Our aim will be to act just as He would if He was in our places, regardless of immediate results. In other words, we propose to follow Jesus' steps as closely and as literally as we believe He taught His disciples to do."

The people glanced at one another in astonishment. It was not like Henry Maxwell to define Christian discipleship in this way. His proposition was understood well enough, but there was a great difference of opinion as to the application of Jesus' teaching and example.

Mr. Maxwell calmly closed the service with a brief prayer, and the organist began his postlude immediately after the benediction. After several minutes the minister asked all who expected to remain to pass into the lecture room that joined the large room on the side. He was himself detained at the front of the church, and when he finally walked over to the lecture room entrance and went in, he was amazed to see the people who were there. He had hardly expected that so many were ready to enter into such a literal testing of their Christian discipleship. There were perhaps fifty present, among them Rachel Winslow and Virginia Page, Mr. Norman, President Marsh, Alexander Powers, Milton Wright, Dr. West, and Jasper Chase.

He closed the door of the lecture room and went and stood before the little group, his face pale and his lips trembling with genuine emotion. Henry Maxwell was conscious of a great upheaval in his definition of Christian discipleship, and he was moved with a depth of feeling he could not measure.

He asked them all to pray with him. And almost with the first syllable he uttered, there was a distinct presence of the Spirit felt by them all. The room filled with it as plainly as if it had been visible. When the prayer closed there was a silence that lasted several moments. All the heads were bowed. Henry Maxwell's face was wet with tears. He spoke very quietly. "The experience I have been through since last Sunday has left me so dissatisfied with my previous definition of Christian discipleship that I am compelled to take this action. I did not dare begin it alone. Do we understand fully what we have undertaken?"

"I want to ask a question," said Rachel Winslow. Her face glowed with a beauty that no physical loveliness could ever create. "I am a little in doubt as to the source of our knowledge concerning what Jesus would do. Who is to decide for me just what He would do in my case? There are many perplexing questions in our civilization that are not mentioned in the teachings of Jesus. How am I going to tell what He would do?"

"There is no way that I know of," replied the pastor, "except as we study Jesus through the medium of the Holy Spirit. You remember what Christ said speaking to His disciples about the Holy Spirit in John 16:13: 'Howbeit when he, the Spirit of truth, is come, he will guide you into all truth.' There is no other test that I know of. We shall all have to decide what Jesus would do after going to that source of knowledge."

"What if others say of us, when we do certain things, that Jesus would not do so?" asked the superintendent of railroads.

"We cannot prevent that. But we must be absolutely honest with ourselves. The standard of Christian action cannot vary in most of our acts. When it comes to a genuine, honest, enlightened following of Jesus' steps, I cannot believe there will be any confusion either in our own minds or in the judgment of others. But we need to remember this great fact. After we have asked the Spirit to tell us what Jesus would do and have received an answer to it, we are to act regardless of the results to ourselves. Is that understood?"

All the faces in the room were raised toward the minister in solemn assent.

They agreed to report to one another every week the result of their experiences in following Jesus this way. Henry Maxwell prayed again, and the Spirit's presence was again evident. Every head remained bowed a long time. They went away finally in silence.

Chapter 3

Edward Norman, editor of the Raymond *Daily News,* sat in his office room Monday morning and faced a new world of action. He had made his pledge in good faith to do everything after asking, "What would Jesus do?" and, as he supposed, with his eyes open to all the possible results. But as the regular life of the paper started on another week's rush and whirl of activity, he confronted it with a degree of hesitation and a feeling nearly akin to fear.

He had come down to the office very early and for a few minutes was by himself. He rose and shut his door, and then did what he had not done for years. He knelt down by his desk and prayed for the Divine Presence and wisdom to direct him.

He rose with the day before him and his promise distinct and clear in his mind. He opened his door and began the routine of the office work by writing an editorial. The *Daily News* was an evening paper, and Norman usually completed his leading editorial before nine o'clock.

Fifteen minutes later the managing editor called out from his desk in the adjoining room, "Here's this press report of yesterday's prizefight at the Resort. It will make up three and a half columns. I suppose it all goes in?"

"Yes—no. Let me see it."

Norman took the typewritten matter just as it came from the telegraph editor and ran over it carefully. Then he laid the sheets down on his desk and did some very hard thinking.

"We won't run this today," he said finally.

The managing editor stood in the doorway between the two rooms. "What did you say?"

"Leave it out. We won't use it."

"But—" The managing editor stared at Norman as if the man were out of his mind.

"I don't think, Clark, that it ought to be printed, and that's the end of it," said Norman, looking up from his desk.

Clark seldom had any words with the chief. The circumstances now, however, seemed to be so extraordinary that he could not help expressing himself.

"Do you mean that the paper is to go to press without a word of the prizefight in it?"

"Yes. That's what I mean."

"But it's unheard of. What will our subscribers say? Why, it is simply—" Clark paused, unable to find words to say what he thought.

Norman looked at Clark thoughtfully. The two men had never talked together on religious matters, although they had been associated on the paper for several years.

"Come in here a minute, Clark, and shut the door." Clark came in, and the two men faced each other alone.

Norman did not speak for a minute. Then he said abruptly, "Clark, if Christ were editor of a daily paper, do you honestly think He would print three and a half columns of prizefight in it?"

"No, I don't suppose He would."

"Well, that's my only reason for shutting this account out of the *News*. I have decided not to do a thing in connection with the paper for a whole year that I honestly believe Jesus would not do."

Clark could not have looked more amazed if the chief had suddenly gone crazy. "What effect will that have on the paper?" he finally managed to ask in a faint voice.

"What do you think?" asked Norman with a keen glance.

"I think it will ruin the paper," replied Clark promptly. "It's too ideal. You can't make it pay. If you shut out this prizefight report, you will lose hundreds of subscribers."

Norman spoke gently but firmly. "Clark, in your honest opinion, would you say that the highest, best law for a man to live by was contained in asking the question, 'What would Jesus do?' and then

15

doing it regardless of results?"

Clark turned red and moved uneasily in his chair before he answered the editor's question. "Why—yes—I suppose if you put it on the ground of what men ought to do, there is no other standard of conduct. But to succeed in the newspaper business, we have got to conform to custom and the recognized methods of society."

"Do you mean that we can't run the paper strictly on Christian principles and make it succeed?"

"Yes, that's just what I mean. We'll go bankrupt in thirty days."

Norman did not reply at once. He was very thoughtful. "We shall have occasion to talk this over again, Clark. Meanwhile I think we ought to understand each other frankly. I shall continue to do as I have pledged in the belief that not only can we succeed, but we can succeed better than we ever did."

Clark rose. "The report does not go in?"

"It does not. There is plenty of good material to take its place, and you know what it is."

Clark hesitated. "Are you going to say anything about the absence of the report?"

"No, let the paper go to press as if there had been no such thing as a prizefight yesterday."

When the *Daily News* came out that evening, it carried to its subscribers a distinct sensation. The presence of the report of the prizefight could not have produced anything equal to the effect of its omission. Hundreds of men in the hotels and stores downtown, as well as regular subscribers, eagerly opened the paper and searched it through for the account of the great fight; not finding it, they rushed to the newsstands and bought other papers. That evening, as Mr. Norman walked out of the office and went home, he could not avoid that constant query, "Would Jesus have done it?" It was not so much with reference to this specific transaction as to the entire motive that had urged him on since he had made the promise.

He came to the conclusion that Jesus would have done either what he did or something similar in order to be free from any possible feeling of injustice.

Chapter 4

During the week Norman received numerous letters commenting on the absence of the account of the prizefight from the *News*.

Dear Sir—I want a journal that is up to the times, progressive, and enterprising, supplying the public demand at all points. The recent freak of your paper in refusing to print the account of the famous contest at the Resort has decided me finally to change my paper. Please discontinue it.

From one of Norman's old friends, an editor of a daily in a nearby town:

Dear Ed.—What is this sensation you have given the people of your burg? What new policy have you taken up? Hope you don't intend to try the "Reform Business" through the avenue of the press. It's dangerous to experiment much along that line. Take my advice and stick to the enterprising modern methods you have made so successful for the News.

My Dear Mr. Norman,
I hasten to write you a note of appreciation for the evident carrying out of your promise. It is a splendid beginning, and no one feels the value of it more than I do. I know something of what it will cost you, but not all.

Your pastor,
Henry Maxwell

One other letter he opened immediately after reading this:

> *Dear Sir—At the expiration of my advertising limit, you will do me the favor not to continue it as you have done heretofore. I enclose check for payment in full and shall consider my account with your paper closed after date.*

It was signed by one of the largest dealers in tobacco in the city. His usual ad was a column of conspicuous advertising, for a very large price.

After a moment he took up a copy of his paper and looked through the advertising columns. He had not considered this before. As he glanced over the columns, he could not escape the conviction that his Master could not permit some of them in his paper.

As a member of a church and a respected citizen, he had incurred no special censure because the saloon men advertised in his columns. No one thought anything about it. It was all legitimate business. He was simply doing what every other businessman in Raymond did. And it was one of the best-paying sources of revenue. What would the paper do if it cut these out? Could it live? That was the question. But—was that the question after all? "What would Jesus do?" That was the question he was answering, or trying to answer, this week. Edward Norman asked it honestly, and after a prayer for help and wisdom, he asked Clark to come into the office.

"Clark," said Norman, speaking slowly and carefully, "I've been looking at our advertising columns and have decided to dispense with some of the matter as soon as the contracts run out. I wish you would notify the advertising agent not to solicit or renew the ads that I have marked here."

He handed the paper with the marked places over to Clark, who took it and looked over the columns with a very serious air.

"This will mean a great loss to the *News*. How long do you think you can keep this sort of thing up?"

"Clark, do you think if Jesus were the editor and proprietor of a daily paper in Raymond, He would permit advertisements of whiskey and tobacco in it?"

"Well—no—I don't suppose He would. But newspapers can't be run on any such basis."

"Why not?" asked Norman quietly.

"Because they will lose more money than they make, that's all!" Clark spoke out with an irritation that he really felt. "We shall certainly bankrupt the paper with this sort of business policy."

"Do you think so?" Norman asked the question not as if he expected an answer, but simply as if he were talking with himself. After a pause he said, "You may direct Marks to do as I have said. I cannot believe that by any kind of reasoning we could reach a conclusion justifying our Lord in the advertisement of whiskey and tobacco in a newspaper. I feel a conviction in regard to these that cannot be silenced."

Clark went back to his desk feeling as if he had been in the presence of a very peculiar person. What would become of business if this standard were adopted? It would upset every custom and introduce endless confusion. It was simply foolishness. It was downright idiocy.

❧

When Edward Norman came down to the office Friday morning, he was confronted with the usual program for the Sunday morning edition. The *News* was one of the few evening papers in Raymond to issue a Sunday edition, and it had always been remarkably successful financially. It had always been welcomed by all the subscribers, church members and all, as a Sunday morning necessity.

Edward Norman now put to himself the question, "What would Jesus do?" If He were editor of a paper, would He deliberately plan to put into the homes of all the church people and Christians of Raymond such a collection of reading matter on the one day in the week that ought to be given up to something better and holier? Taking everything into account, would Jesus edit a Sunday morning paper? No matter whether it paid. That was not the question. As a matter of fact, the Sunday *News* paid so well that it would be a direct loss of thousands of dollars to discontinue it.

He was honestly perplexed by the question. So much was involved in the discontinuance of the Sunday edition that for the first time he almost decided to refuse to be guided by the standard of Jesus' probable action. As he sat there surrounded by the usual quantity of material for the Sunday edition, he reached some definite conclusions. And among them was a determination to call in the force of the paper and frankly state his motive and purpose.

He sent word for all his employees to come into the mailing room. The men came in curiously and perched around on the tables and counters.

"I called you in here to let you know my further plans for the *News*. I understand very well that you consider some things I have already done as very strange. I wish to state my motive in doing what I have done."

Here he told the men what he had already told Clark, and they stared as Clark had done and looked as painfully conscious.

"Now, in acting on this standard of conduct, I have reached a conclusion which will, no doubt, cause some surprise.

"I have decided that the Sunday morning edition of the *News* shall be discontinued after next Sunday's issue. I shall state in that issue my reasons for discontinuing. In order to make up to the subscribers the amount of reading matter they may suppose themselves entitled to, we can issue a double number on Saturday, as is done by many evening papers that make no attempt at a Sunday edition. I am convinced that from a Christian point of view our Sunday morning paper has done more harm than good. I do not believe that Jesus would be responsible for it if He were in my place today. It will take some trouble to arrange the details caused by this change with the advertisers and subscribers. That is for me to look after. So far as I can see, the loss will fall on myself. Neither the reporters nor the pressmen need make any particular changes in their plans."

He looked around the room and no one spoke. He was struck for the first time in his life with the fact that in all the years of his newspaper life, he had never had the force of the paper together in this way. Would Jesus do that?

The vague picture that came up in the mailing room would not fade away when he had gone into his office and the men had gone back to their places with wonder in their looks and questions of all sorts on their tongues as they talked over the editor's remarkable actions.

Clark came in and had a long, serious talk with his chief, almost reaching the point of resigning his place. Norman guarded himself carefully. Every minute of the interview was painful to him, but he felt more than ever the necessity of doing the Christlike thing. Clark was a very valuable man. It would be difficult to fill his place.

"Mr. Norman, I don't understand you. You are not the same man this week that I always knew before."

"I don't know myself either, Clark. But I was never more convinced of final success and power for the paper. Will you stay with the *News*?"

Clark hesitated a moment and finally said yes.

Chapter 5

The next Sunday morning Henry Maxwell's church was again crowded.

Henry Maxwell faced it all with a calmness that indicated an unusual strength and purpose. While his prayers were very helpful, his sermon was not so easy to describe. He did not preach as he had done two Sundays before.

He agonized over his preparation for his sermon, and yet he knew he had not been able to fit his message into his ideal of the Christ. Nevertheless, no one in the First Church could remember ever hearing such a sermon before. There was in it rebuke for sin— things that First Church never heard rebuked this way before. And there was a love of his people that gathered new force as the sermon went on. When it was finished there were those who said in their hearts, "The Spirit moved that sermon." Then Rachel Winslow rose to sing, this time after the sermon, by Mr. Maxwell's request. Today there was no lack of power in her grand voice, but there was an added element of humility and purity that the audience noted.

Before the service closed, Mr. Maxwell asked those who had remained the week before to stay again for a few moments of consultation, and welcomed any others who were willing to make the pledge at that time. When he went into the lecture room, it was almost filled. As before, Maxwell asked them to pray with him, and again a distinct answer came from the presence of the divine Spirit. There was no doubt in the minds of any present that what they purposed to do was clearly in line with the divine will. There was a feeling of fellowship such as they had never known in their church membership. Jasper Chase said, "I have been puzzled several times during the week to know just what Jesus would do. It is not always an easy question to answer."

"I think perhaps I find it specially difficult to answer that question on account of my money," Virginia Page said. "Our Lord never owned any property, and there is nothing in His example to guide me in the use of mine." Virginia smiled slightly. "What I am trying to discover is a principle that will enable me to come to the nearest possible to His action as it ought to influence the entire course of my life so far as my wealth and its use are concerned."

"That will take time," said the minister slowly.

Milton Wright told how he was gradually working out a plan for his business relations with his employees, and it was opening up a new world to him and to them.

There was almost general consent over the fact that the application of the Christ spirit and practice to the everyday life required a knowledge of Him and an insight into His motives that most of them did not yet possess.

When they finally adjourned after a silent prayer that marked with growing power the Divine Presence, they went away discussing earnestly their difficulties and seeking light from one another.

After the others had gone, Alexander Powers spoke to his pastor. "I want you to come down to the shops tomorrow and see my plan and talk to the men. Somehow I feel as if you could get nearer to them than anyone else just now."

How was he fitted to stand before two or three hundred workingmen and give them a message? Yet in the moment of his weakness, he asked the question, "What would Jesus do?" That was an end to the discussion.

He went down the next day and found Mr. Powers in his office. The superintendent said, "Come upstairs, and I'll show you what I've been trying to do."

They went through the machine shop, climbed a long flight of stairs, and entered a very large, empty room that had once been used by the company for a storeroom.

"My plan is to provide a good place where the men can come

up and eat their noon lunch, and give them, two or three times a week, the privilege of a fifteen-minute talk on some subject that will be a real help to them in their lives."

Maxwell asked if the men would come for any such purpose.

"Yes, they'll come. They are among the most intelligent workingmen in the country today. But they are, as a whole, entirely removed from church influence. I asked, 'What would Jesus do?' and it seemed to me He would begin to act in some way to add more physical and spiritual comfort to the lives of these men. I have asked them to come up at noon and see the place, and I'll tell them something about it. I want you to speak to them, too."

There were a dozen rude benches and tables in the room, and when the noon whistle sounded, about three hundred men poured upstairs from the machine shops below and, seating themselves at the tables, began to eat their lunch.

At about twenty minutes to one, Mr. Powers told the men what he had in mind. He spoke very simply, like one who understands thoroughly the character of his audience, and then introduced the Reverend Henry Maxwell of the First Church, his pastor, who had consented to speak a few minutes.

Maxwell would never forget the feeling with which, for the first time, he stood before the grimy-faced audience of workingmen. Like hundreds of other ministers, he had never spoken to any gatherings except those made up of people of his own class in the sense that they were familiar in their dress and education and habits. This was a new world to him, and nothing but his new rule of conduct could have made possible his message and its effect.

Alexander Powers went back to his desk that afternoon with a glow of satisfaction. After all, he wanted to do as Jesus would, he said to himself.

It was nearly four o'clock when he opened one of the company's long envelopes. He ran over the first page of typewritten matter in his usual quick, businesslike manner before he saw that what he was reading was not intended for his office but for the superintendent of the freight department.

He turned over a page mechanically. Before he knew it, he was in possession of evidence that conclusively proved that the company was engaged in a systematic violation of the Interstate Commerce Laws of the United States and the new state laws.

He dropped the papers on his desk as if they were poison, and instantly the question flashed across his mind, "What would Jesus do?"

He had known in a more or less definite way that this had been going on. But he was not in a position to prove anything directly, and he had regarded it as a matter that did not concern him at all. Now the papers before him revealed the entire affair.

If he came out against this lawlessness as a witness, it would drag him into courts, his motives would be misunderstood, and the whole thing would end in his disgrace and the loss of his position. Surely it was none of his business. He could easily get the papers back to the freight department and no one would be the wiser. Let the iniquity go on. Let the law be defied. What was it to him? He would work out his plans for bettering the condition of his men. What more could a man do in this railroad business when there was so much going on anyway that made it impossible to live by the Christian standard? But what would Jesus do if He knew the facts? Day wore into evening as Alexander Powers pondered the question. At six o'clock the whistle blew, the engine slowed, and the men dropped their tools and ran for the blockhouse.

Powers waited until he heard the last man clock out. Then he knelt and buried his face in his hands as he bowed his head upon the papers on his desk.

Chapter 6

After the Sunday meeting, Virginia Page asked Rachel Winslow to come and lunch with her at noon the next day. There they continued their conversation.

"The fact is," Rachel said, "I cannot reconcile this offer with my judgment of what Christ would do."

"What will you do, then?" asked Virginia with great interest.

"I don't know yet, but I have decided to refuse this offer."

Rachel picked up the letter lying in her lap and ran over its contents again. It was from the manager of a comic opera, offering her a place with a large traveling company. The salary was a very large figure, and the prospect was flattering.

"The concert offer is harder to decide," Rachel went on thoughtfully. "Here is a reputable company, and I would travel with people of good reputation. I'm asked to go as one of the company and sing leading soprano. The salary is guaranteed to be $200 a month for the season. But I don't feel satisfied that Jesus would go. What do you think?"

"You mustn't ask me to decide for you," replied Virginia with a sad smile. "Mr. Maxwell was right when he said we must each one of us decide according to the judgment we feel for ourselves to be Christlike."

Rachel rose and walked over to the window and looked out. Virginia came and stood by her. The street was crowded with life, and the two young women looked at it silently for a moment.

Suddenly Virginia broke out: "Rachel, I've been educated in one of the most expensive schools in America and launched into society as an heiress. I'm perfectly well; I can do as I please. I can gratify almost any want or desire; and yet when I honestly try to imagine Jesus living the life I have lived and am expected to live, and doing for the rest of my life what thousands of other rich people do, I am under condemnation for being one of the most wicked, selfish, useless creatures in all the world."

Virginia turned away and walked up and down the room. Rachel watched her and could not repress the rising tide of her own growing definition of discipleship. She, too, was in sound health, was conscious of her great powers as a singer, and knew that if she went out into public life, she could make a great deal of money and become well-known. When lunch was announced, they were joined by Virginia's grandmother, Madam Page, a handsome, stately woman of sixty-five, and Virginia's brother, Rollin, a young man who spent most of his time at one of the clubs and had no ambition for anything but a growing admiration for Rachel Winslow.

These three made up the Page family. Virginia's father had been a banker and grain speculator. Her mother had died ten years before, her father within the past year. The grandmother, a Southern woman in birth and training, had all the traditions and feelings that accompany the possession of wealth and social standing that have never been disturbed. She was a shrewd, careful businesswoman of more than average ability. The family property and wealth were invested, in large measure, under her personal care.

Rachel, who had known the family since she was a girl playmate of Virginia's, could not help thinking of what confronted Virginia in her own home when she once decided on the course she honestly believed Jesus would take.

"I understand that you are going on the stage, Miss Winslow. We shall all be delighted, I'm sure," said Rollin during the conversation.

Rachel answered quietly, "You're mistaken. I'm not going on the stage."

"It's a great pity. You'd make a hit. Everybody is talking about your singing."

Rachel flushed with genuine anger. Before she could say anything, Virginia broke in: "Whom do you mean by 'everybody'?"

"Whom? I mean all the people who hear Miss Winslow on Sundays. It's a great pity, I say, that the general public outside of Raymond cannot hear her voice."

"Let us talk about something else," said Rachel a little sharply.

Madam Page glanced at her and spoke with a gentle courtesy. "My dear, we are all curious to know something of your plans. We claim the right from old acquaintance, you know; and Virginia has already told us of your concert company offer."

"I understand that, Madam Page," Rachel replied hastily. "I have decided not to accept."

What Rollin Page had said and his manner in saying it had hastened her decision in the matter.

"Would you mind telling us your reasons for refusing the offer? It looks like a great opportunity for a young girl like you. A voice like yours belongs to a larger audience than Raymond and the First Church."

"I have no other reason than a conviction that Jesus Christ would do the same thing," she said, looking into Madam Page's eyes with a clear, earnest gaze.

Madam Page turned red and Rollin stared.

Before her grandmother could say anything, Virginia spoke. Her rising color showed how she was stirred. "Grandmother, you know we promised to make that the standard of our conduct for a year. We have not been able to arrive at our decisions very rapidly. The difficulty in knowing what Jesus would do has perplexed Rachel and me a good deal."

Madam Page looked sharply at Virginia before she said anything. "Mr. Maxwell's statement is visionary and absurd. I have nothing to say about Miss Winslow's affairs, but"—she paused and continued with a sharpness that was new to Rachel—"I hope you have no foolish notions in this matter, Virginia."

"I have a great many notions," replied Virginia quietly. "Whether they are foolish or not depends upon my right understanding of what He would do."

"What you have promised, in a spirit of false emotion, is

impossible of performance."

"Do you mean, Grandmother, that we cannot possibly act as our Lord would? Or do you mean that, if we try to, we shall offend the customs and prejudices of society?" asked Virginia.

"It is not required! It is not necessary! Besides, how can you act with any—" Madam Page paused, broke off her sentence, and then turned to Rachel. "What will your mother say to your decision?"

"I don't know what Mother will say yet," Rachel answered, with a great shrinking from trying to give her mother's probable answer. If there was a woman in all Raymond with great ambitions for her daughter's success as a singer, Mrs. Winslow was that woman.

"Oh! You will see it in a different light after wiser thought of it. My dear," continued Madam Page, rising from the table, "you will live to regret it if you do not accept the concert company's offer or something like it."

Chapter 7

Rachel was glad to escape and be by herself to carefully think out a plan that was slowly forming in her mind. But before she had walked two blocks, she was annoyed to find Rollin Page walking beside her.

"Sorry to disturb your thoughts, Miss Winslow, but I happened to be going your way. In fact, I've been walking here for a whole block, and you haven't objected."

"I did not see you," said Rachel briefly.

She had known Rollin as a boy. She was used to his direct attempts at compliments and was sometimes amused by them. Today she honestly wished him anywhere else.

"Do you ever think of me, Miss Winslow?" asked Rollin after a pause.

"Oh yes, quite often!" said Rachel with a smile.

"Are you thinking of me now?"

"Do you want me to be absolutely truthful?"

"Of course."

"Then I was thinking that I wished you were not here."

Rollin bit his lip and looked gloomy. "Now look here, Rachel, you know how I feel. You used to like me a little, you know."

"Did I? Of course we used to get on very well as boy and girl. But we are older now."

Rachel spoke in a light, easy way, still somewhat preoccupied with her plan.

They walked along in silence a little way. The avenue was full of people. Among them was Jasper Chase, who bowed as Rachel and Rollin went by. Rachel colored in spite of herself.

"You know well enough, Rachel, how I feel toward you. I could make you happy. I've loved you a good many years—"

"Why, how old do you think I am?" broke in Rachel with a nervous laugh, shaken out of her usual poise of manner.

"You know what I mean," went on Rollin doggedly. "And you have no right to laugh at me just because I want you to marry me."

"I'm not! But it is useless for you to speak, Rollin," said Rachel after a little hesitation. "It is impossible."

"Would—that is—do you think—if you gave me time, I would—"

"No!" said Rachel. She spoke firmly.

They walked on for some time without a word. As they turned off the avenue into one of the quieter streets, Rollin spoke suddenly and with more manliness than he had yet shown. There was a distinct note of dignity in his voice that was new to Rachel.

"Miss Winslow, I ask you to be my wife. Is there any hope for me that you will ever consent?"

"None in the least." Rachel spoke decidedly.

"Will you tell me why?"

"Because I do not feel toward you as a woman ought to feel toward the man she marries."

"In other words, you do not love me?"

"I do not and I cannot."

"Why?" That was another question, and Rachel was a little surprised that he should ask it. "Tell me. You can't hurt me more than you have already."

"Well, I do not and I cannot love you because you have no purpose in life. What do you ever do to make the world better? You spend your time in club life, in amusements, in travel, in luxury. What is there in such a life to attract a woman?"

"Not much, I guess," said Rollin with a bitter laugh. "Still, I don't know that I'm any worse than the rest of the men around me."

He suddenly stopped, took off his hat, bowed gravely, and turned back. Rachel went on home and hurried into her room, disturbed in many ways.

When she had time to think it all over, she found herself condemned by the very judgment she had passed on Rollin Page. What purpose had she in life? There was a fortune in her voice. She knew it, not necessarily as a matter of personal pride or professional egotism, but simply as a fact. And she was obliged to acknowledge that until two weeks ago she had purposed to use her voice to make money and win admiration and applause. Was that a much higher purpose, after all, than Rollin Page lived for?

After much thought, she finally resolved to have a frank talk with her mother. Mrs. Winslow was a large, handsome woman, fond of much company, ambitious for distinction in society, and devoted to the success of her children. Rachel's father, like Virginia's, had died while the family was abroad. Like Virginia, she found herself, under her present rule of conduct, in complete antagonism with her own immediate home circle.

Rachel came at once to the point. "Mother, I have decided not to go out with the company."

Mrs. Winslow said nothing but waited for Rachel to go on.

"You know the promise I made two weeks ago?"

"Mr. Maxwell's promise?"

"No, mine."

"What has that to do with your decision in the concert company matter?"

"It has everything to do with it. After asking, 'What would Jesus do?' and going to the source of authority for wisdom, I'm obliged to say that I do not believe He would make that use of my voice."

"Why? Is there anything wrong about such a career?"

"No, I don't know that I can say there is. As I look at it, I have a conviction that Jesus would do something else."

"What else?"

"Something that will serve humanity where it most needs the service of song. Something that will satisfy me when I ask, 'What would Jesus do?' I have been unable, since I made my promise two weeks ago, to imagine Jesus joining a concert company to do what I should do and live the life I should have to live if I joined it."

Rachel spoke with a vigor and earnestness that surprised her mother. But Mrs. Winslow was angry now.

"It is simply absurd! Rachel, you are a fanatic!" Mrs. Winslow rose and then sat down again. With a great effort she composed herself. "What do you intend to do, then?"

"I shall continue to sing for the time being in the church. During the week I am going to sing at the White Cross meetings, down in the Rectangle."

"What? Rachel Winslow! Do you know what you are saying? Do you know what sort of people those are down there?"

For a moment Rachel shrank back and was silent. Then she spoke firmly. "I know very well. Mr. and Mrs. Gray have been working there several weeks. I learned only this morning that they want singers from the churches to help them in their meetings."

Rachel cried out with the first passionate utterance she had yet used. "What have we done all our lives for the suffering, sinning side of Raymond? How much have we denied ourselves or given of our personal ease and pleasure to bless the place in which we live or imitate the life of the Savior of the world? I want to do something that will cost me something in the way of sacrifice."

"Are you preaching at me?" asked Mrs. Winslow slowly.

Rachel rose. "No. I am preaching at myself," she replied gently. She paused a moment as if she thought her mother would say something more, and then went out of the room.

❖

About seven o'clock Virginia and her uncle, Dr. West, appeared, and together the three started for the scene of the White Cross meetings.

The Rectangle, close by the railroad shops and the packinghouses, was the most notorious district in Raymond. The great slum and tenement district was shut in by rows of saloons, gambling halls, and cheap, dirty boarding and lodging houses.

Into this heart of the coarse part of the sin of Raymond, the traveling evangelist and his brave little wife had pitched a good-sized tent and begun meetings.

It was after eight o'clock when Alexander Powers opened the door of his office and started for home. He was going to take a car at the corner of the Rectangle, but he was stirred by a voice coming from the tent.

How did Rachel Winslow happen to be down here? Her voice struck through his consciousness of struggle over his own question that had sent him into the Divine Presence for an answer, though he had not yet reached a conclusion.

Several windows nearby went up. Some men quarreling near a saloon stopped and listened. Other figures walked rapidly in the direction of the Rectangle and the tent.

Surely Rachel Winslow had never sung like that in the First Church. What was it she was singing?

"Where He leads me I will follow,
Where He leads me I will follow,
Where He leads me I will follow,
I'll go with Him, with Him
All the way!"

After a minute of indecision the superintendent went on to the corner and took the car for his home. But before he was out of the sound of Rachel's voice, he had settled for himself the question of what Jesus would do.

Chapter 8

Henry Maxwell paced his study back and forth, thinking out the subject of his Wednesday evening service. After a while he sat down at his desk and drew a large piece of paper toward him. Then he wrote in large letters the following:

Things Jesus Would Probably Do in This Parish

1. *Live in a simple, plain manner.*
2. *Preach fearlessly to the hypocrites in the church.*
3. *Show in some practical form His sympathy and love for all people.*
4. *Identify Himself with the great causes of humanity in some personal way that would call for self-denial and suffering.*
5. *Preach against the saloon in Raymond.*
6. *Become known as a friend and companion of the sinful people in the Rectangle.*
7. *Give up the summer trip to Europe this year.*

He was conscious that his outline of Jesus' probable action painfully lacked depth and power, but he searched for concrete shapes into which he might cast his thought of Jesus' conduct. Nearly every point he'd put down meant a complete overturning of his custom and habit of years in the ministry. But still he searched deeper for sources of the Christlike spirit. A servant broke into his thoughts, announcing a caller, Mr. Gray. He immediately stated the reason for his call.

"You have heard what a wonderful meeting we had Monday

night and last night. Miss Winslow has done more with her voice than I could do, and the tent won't hold the people."

Maxwell nodded.

"But I came to ask if you could come down tonight and preach. I am suffering from a severe cold. I know it is asking a good deal from such a busy man. But if you can't come, say so frankly, and I'll try somewhere else."

"It's my regular prayer meeting night," began Henry Maxwell. Then he flushed and added, "I shall be able to arrange it in some way so as to come down."

Gray thanked him earnestly and rose to go.

"Won't you stay a minute, Gray, and let us have a prayer together?"

So the two men knelt together in the study. Gray was touched to tears as Henry Maxwell begged for wisdom and strength to speak a message to the people in the Rectangle.

The night was mild and the sides of the tent were up and a great border of faces stretched around, looking in and forming part of the audience. After the singing and a prayer by one of the city pastors who was present, Gray stated the reason for his inability to speak and in his simple manner turned the service over to "Brother Maxwell, of the First Church."

Henry Maxwell stood up, and a great wave of actual terror went over him. This was not like preaching to the well-dressed, respectable, good-mannered people up on the boulevard. He began to speak, but the crowd was unruly. He turned to Rachel with a sad smile.

"Sing something, Miss Winslow. They will listen to you," he said, and then sat down and covered his face with his hands.

Before Rachel finished the verse, the Rectangle lay like some wild beast at her feet, and she sang it into harmlessness.

When the song was over, Maxwell rose again. This time he felt calmer. What would Jesus do? He spoke as he thought once he never could speak. Who were these people? They were immortal souls. What was Christianity? A calling of sinners, not the righteous, to repentance. How would Jesus speak? What would He say? He could not tell all that His message would include, but he felt sure of a part of it. And in that certainty he spoke on.

When the meeting closed, the people rapidly melted away from the tent, and the saloons, which had been experiencing a dull season while the meetings progressed, again drove a thriving trade. Maxwell and his little party, including Virginia, Rachel, and Jasper Chase, walked down past the row of saloons and dens until they reached the corner where the cars passed.

"This is a terrible spot," said the minister as he stood waiting for their car. "I never realized that Raymond had such a festering sore. It does not seem possible that this is a city full of Christian disciples."

"Do you think anyone can ever remove this great curse of drink?" asked Jasper.

"I have thought lately as never before of what Christian people might do to remove the curse of the saloon. Why don't we all act together against it? What would Jesus do? Would He keep silent? Would He vote to license these causes of crime and death?"

He talked to himself more than to the others. He remembered that he had always voted for license, and so had nearly all his church members. What would Jesus do? Would the Master preach and act against the saloon if He lived today? Suppose it was not popular to preach against license? Suppose the Christian people thought it was all that could be done to license the evil and so get revenue from the necessary sin? Or suppose the church members themselves owned the property where the saloons stood—what then?

He went up into his study the next morning with that question only partly answered. He was still thinking of it and reaching certain real conclusions when the evening *News* came. His wife brought it up and sat down a few minutes while he read to her.

The evening *News* was at present the most sensational paper in Raymond. It no longer printed accounts of crime with detailed descriptions or scandals in private life. The advertisements of liquor and tobacco were dropped, together with certain others of a questionable character. Now the character of the editorials was creating the greatest excitement. Monday's editorial was headed:

THE MORAL SIDE OF POLITICAL QUESTIONS

The editor of the News has always advocated the principles of the great political party at present in power and has discussed all political questions from the standpoint of expedience, or of belief in the party as opposed to other political organizations. From now on, the first question asked in this office will be, "Is this measure in accordance with the spirit and teachings of Jesus as the author of the greatest standard of life known to men?" The moral side of every political question will be considered its most important side, and the ground will be distinctly taken that nations as well as individuals are under the same law to do all things to the glory of God as the first rule of action.

The same principle will be applied toward candidates for places of responsibility and trust in the republic. The editor of the News will do all in his power to bring the best men into power, and will not knowingly help to support for office any candidate who is unworthy, no matter how much he may be endorsed by the party. The first question asked about the man and about the measures will be, "Is he the right man for the place?" "Is he a good man with ability?" "Is the measure right?"

As Maxwell read to his wife, he could see in almost every column evidences of Norman's conscientious obedience to his promise. There was an absence of slangy, sensational scare heads. The reading matter under the headlines was in perfect keeping with them. He noticed in two columns that the reporters' names appeared signed at the bottom. And there was a distinct advance in the dignity and style of their contributions.

Maxwell suddenly paused. His wife looked up from some work she was doing. He was reading something with the utmost interest. "Listen to this, Mary," he said after a moment while his lip trembled:

This morning Alexander Powers, superintendent of the L&T RR shops in this city, handed in his resignation to the road, and gave as his reason the fact that certain proofs had fallen into his hands of the violation of the Interstate Commerce Law and state law, which has recently been framed to prevent and punish railroad pooling for the benefit of certain favored shippers. Mr. Powers has placed his evidence against the company in the hands of the Commission and it is now for them to take action.

The News wishes to express itself on this action of Mr. Powers. In the first place, he has nothing to gain by it. He has lost a very valuable place voluntarily, when by keeping silent he might have retained it. In the second place, we believe his action ought to receive the approval of all thoughtful, honest citizens who believe in seeing law obeyed and lawbreakers brought to justice. In our judgment, Mr. Powers did the only thing that a Christian man could do. He has rendered brave and useful service to the state and the general public. It is not always an easy matter to determine the relations that exist between the individual citizen and his fixed duty to the public. In this case, there is no doubt in our minds that the step which Mr. Powers has taken commends itself to everyone who believes in law and its enforcement. Mr. Powers has done all that a loyal, patriotic citizen could do. It now remains for the Commission to act upon his evidence, which, we understand, is overwhelming proof of the lawlessness of the L&T. Let the law be enforced, no matter who the persons may be who have been guilty.

Chapter 9

Henry Maxwell finished reading and dropped the paper. "I must go and see Powers. This is the result of his promise."

Maxwell walked over to the next block where Superintendent Powers lived. To his relief, Powers himself came to the door.

The two men shook hands silently. They instantly understood each other without words. "What are you going to do?" Henry Maxwell asked after they had talked over the facts in the case.

"I have no plans yet. I can go back to my old work as a telegraph operator. My family will not suffer, except in a social way."

Powers spoke calmly and sadly. "There is one matter I wish you would see to—the work begun at the shops. So far as I know, the company will not object to that going on. Will you see that my plan is carried out?"

"Yes," replied Henry Maxwell. Before he went away, he and the superintendent had a prayer together.

As Maxwell thought of Edward Norman and Rachel and Mr. Powers, and of the results that had already come from their actions, he could not help a feeling of intense interest in the probable effect if all the persons in the First Church who had made the pledge faithfully kept it. The next morning the president of the Endeavor Society of his church called to see him.

"I thought," said young Morris, coming at once to his errand, "that you might advise me a little. I've been doing reporter work on the morning *Sentinel* since I graduated last year. Well, last Saturday Mr. Burr asked me to go down the road Sunday morning and get the details of that train robbery at the Junction and write the thing up for the extra edition that came out Monday morning. I refused to go, and Burr gave me my dismissal."

"You kept your promise, Fred."

"Thank you, Mr. Maxwell."

Morris rose to go, and his pastor rose and laid a loving hand on the young man's shoulder.

"What are you going to do, Fred?"

"I don't know yet."

"Why don't you try the *News*?"

"They are all supplied."

Maxwell thought a moment. "Come down to the *News* office with me, and let us see Norman about it."

So a few minutes later, Edward Norman greeted the minister and young Morris, and Maxwell briefly told the cause of the errand.

Norman's keen gaze was softened by a smile that made it winsome. "I want reporters who won't work Sundays. In fact, I am making plans for a special kind of reporting which I believe you can develop because you are in sympathy with what Jesus would do."

He assigned Morris a definite task, and Maxwell started back to his study.

On his way home he passed by one of Milton Wright's stores. He thought he would simply step in and shake hands with his parishioner and bid him Godspeed in what he had heard he was doing to put Christ into his business. But when he went into the office, Wright insisted on detaining him to talk over some of his new plans. "There is no use to disguise the fact, Mr. Maxwell, that I've been compelled to revolutionize the entire method of my business since I made that promise. I came down here Monday morning after that Sunday and asked myself, 'What would Jesus do in His relation to these clerks, bookkeepers, office boys, day men, salesmen? Would He try to establish some sort of personal relation to them different from that which I have sustained all these years?' Then came the question of what that relation would be and what it would lead me to do. I did not see how I could answer it to my satisfaction without getting all my employees together and having a talk with them. So I sent invitations to all of them, and we had a meeting out there in the warehouse Tuesday night. A good many things came out of that meeting. I kept asking, 'What would Jesus do?' and the more I asked it, the farther along it pushed me into the most intimate and loving relations with the men who have worked for me all these years. Every day something new is coming up, and I am right now in the midst of a reconstruction of the motive for conducting business."

Wright eagerly reached up into one of the pigeonholes of his desk and took out a paper.

"I have sketched out what seems to me like a program such as Jesus might go by in a business like mine." He handed the paper to Maxwell.

Henry Maxwell read it over slowly.

What Jesus Would Probably Do
in Milton Wright's Place as a Businessman

1. *The primary purpose of the business is glorifying God.*
2. *He would never regard the money He made as His own.*
3. *His relations with all the persons in His employ would be the most loving and helpful.*
4. *He would never do a single dishonest or questionable thing or try to get the advantage of anyone else.*
5. *The principle of unselfishness and helpfulness in the business would direct all its details.*

Maxwell looked up and met Wright's gaze. "Do you believe you can continue to make your business pay on these lines?"

"I do."

"Does your plan contemplate what is coming to be known as cooperation?"

"Yes, as far as I have gone, it does. I am working on those general principles. I must have time to complete the details."

When Maxwell finally left, he was profoundly impressed with the revolution at work in the business. There was no mistaking the fact that Milton Wright's new relations to his employees were beginning to transform the entire business in a very short time. When Maxwell reached his study, he prayed. Then he began the preparation of a sermon on the subject of the saloon in Raymond, as he now believed Jesus would do.

He had never preached against the saloon before. Nevertheless, he went on with his work, and every sentence he wrote or shaped was preceded with the question, "Would Jesus say that?"

❀

The meetings in the Rectangle had intensified with each night, much of it due to Rachel's singing. It cannot be said that up to that Saturday night there was any appreciable lack of oaths and impurity and heavy drinking. But in spite of itself, there was a yielding to a power it had never measured and did not know well enough to resist beforehand.

Gray had recovered his voice so that by Saturday he was able to speak. Gradually the people had come to understand that this man gave his time and strength to give them a knowledge of a Savior out of a perfectly unselfish love for them. Tonight the great crowd was as quiet as Henry Maxwell's decorous audience ever was. The fringe around the tent was deeper and the saloons were practically empty. The Holy Spirit had come at last, and Gray knew that one of the great prayers of his life was going to be answered.

Rachel's singing was the best that Virginia or Jasper Chase had ever known. They came together again tonight, this time with Dr. West. Virginia was at the organ, Jasper sat on a front seat looking up at Rachel, and the Rectangle swayed as one body toward the platform as she sang:

"Just as I am, without one plea,
But that Thy blood was shed for me,
And that Thou bidst me come to Thee,
O Lamb of God, I come, I come."

Gray stretched out his hand with a gesture of invitation. And down the two aisles of the tent, broken, sinful creatures, men and women, stumbled toward the platform. One woman out of the street was near the organ. Virginia caught the look on her face, and for the first time the thought of what Jesus was to the sinful woman came to her with a suddenness and power that was like nothing but a new birth. Virginia left the organ, went to her, looked into her face, and caught her hands in her own. The other girl trembled, then fell on her knees sobbing, with her head down upon the back of the rude bench in front of her, still clinging to Virginia. And Virginia, after a moment's hesitation, knelt down by her, and the two heads were bowed close together.

When the people had crowded in a double row all about the platform, most of them kneeling and crying, a man in evening dress pushed through the seats and came and knelt down within a few feet of Rachel Winslow, who was still singing softly. And as she turned for a moment and looked in his direction, for a moment her voice faltered. Rollin Page! Then she went on:

"Just as I am, Thou wilt receive,
Wilt welcome, pardon, cleanse, relieve,
Because Thy promise I believe,
O Lamb of God, I come, I come."

Chapter 10

Gray stayed up long into Sunday morning, praying and talking with a little group of converts who in the great experiences of their new life clung to the evangelist with a personal helplessness that made it impossible for him to leave them.

Virginia and her uncle left about eleven o'clock, and Rachel and Jasper Chase went with them as far as the avenue where Virginia lived. Dr. West had walked on a little way with them to his own home, and Rachel and Jasper had then gone on together to her mother's.

Never had her beauty and her strength influenced Jasper Chase as tonight. While she was singing he saw and heard no one else. It was no secret between them that the heroine of Jasper's first novel had been his own ideal of Rachel and the hero in the story was himself. The names and characters were drawn with a subtle skill that revealed to Rachel the fact of his love for her, and she had not been offended. That was nearly a year ago.

Tonight he recalled the scene between them with every inflection and movement vivid in his memory.

"Rachel, you know I love you as my life. I can no longer hide it from you if I would."

Rachel's arm trembled in his. She allowed him to speak and had turned her face neither toward him nor away from him. She looked straight on, and her voice was sad but firm and quiet when she spoke.

"Why do you speak to me now? I cannot bear it—after what we have seen tonight."

"Why—what—"

Rachel withdrew her arm from his but still walked near him. "Rachel! Do you not love me? Is not my love for you as sacred as anything in all of life itself?"

She walked silently for a few steps after that. They passed a streetlamp. Her face was pale and beautiful. He made a movement to clutch her arm, and she moved a little farther from him.

"No," she had replied. "There was a time—. You should not have spoken to me—now."

He had seen in these words his answer. He could not think of pleading with her.

"Sometime—when I am more worthy?" he had asked in a low voice, but she did not seem to hear, and they had parted at her home. No good night had been said.

Now he lashed himself for his foolish precipitance. He had not reckoned on Rachel's tense, passionate absorption of all her feeling in the scenes at the tent that were so new in her mind. When the clock in the First Church struck one, he still sat at his desk staring at the last page of manuscript of his unfinished novel.

❧

Rachel went up to her room and faced her evening's experience with conflicting emotions. Had she ever loved Jasper Chase? Yes. No. But overmastering her emotions Jasper's declaration brought was the response of the wretched creatures in the tent to her singing. The swift, powerful, awesome presence of the Holy Spirit had affected her as never in all her life before.

The moment Jasper spoke her name and she realized that he was telling her of his love, she had felt a sudden revulsion for him. It was not the time to be absorbed in anything less than the divine glory of those conversions. All the time she was singing with the one passion of her soul to touch the conscience of that tent full of sin, Jasper Chase had been unmoved by it except to love her for herself. It gave her a shock as of irreverence on her part as well as on his.

Her mind was busy with the sights she had witnessed in the tent. Those faces, men and women, touched for the first time with the Spirit's glory—what a wonderful thing life was after all! The complete regeneration revealed in the sight of drunken, vile, debauched humanity kneeling down to give itself to a life of purity and Christlikeness was surely a witness to the superhuman in the world! And Rollin Page's face by the side of that miserable wreck out of the gutter!

She recalled Virginia crying with her arms about her brother just before she left the tent, and Mr. Gray kneeling close by, and the girl Virginia had taken into her heart while she whispered something to her before she went out. All these pictures stood out in Rachel's memory now.

"No! No!" she said aloud. "He had no right to speak after all that! I am sure I do not love him—not enough to give him my life!"

❧

The people of Raymond awoke Sunday morning to a growing knowledge of events that were beginning to revolutionize many of the regular, customary habits of the town. Nearly one hundred persons in Henry Maxwell's church had made the pledge to do everything after asking, "What would Jesus do?" The result had been, in many cases, unheard-of actions. As a climax to the week's events had come the spiritual manifestation at the Rectangle, and the announcement of the actual conversion at the tent of nearly fifty of the worst characters in that neighborhood, together with the conversion of Rollin Page, the well-known society and club man.

The First Church of Raymond came to the morning service in a condition that made it quickly sensitive to any large truth. Perhaps nothing had astonished the people more than the great change that had come over the minister since he had proposed to them the imitation of Jesus in conduct. The sermon had become a message. It was brought to them with a love, an earnestness, a passion, a desire, a humility that poured out its enthusiasm about the truth and made the speaker no more prominent than he had to be as the living voice of God. His prayers were unlike any the people had heard before. His great longing to voice the needs and wants of his people made him unmindful of an occasional mistake.

It is certain that he had never prayed so effectively as he did now.

The effect of Henry Maxwell's message this morning owed its power to the unusual fact of his preaching about the saloon at all, together with the events that had stirred the people. He spoke now with a freedom that seemed to measure his complete sense of conviction that Jesus would speak so. At the close he pleaded with the people to remember the new life that had begun at the Rectangle. The regular election of city officers was near at hand. The question of license would be an issue in the election. Was not the most Christian thing they could do to act as citizens in the matter, fight the saloon at the polls, elect good people to the city offices, and clean the municipality? His appeal was stronger at this point than he knew. It is not too much to say that the spiritual tension of the people reached its highest point right there. The imitation of Jesus that had begun with the volunteers in the church was working like leaven in the organization, and Henry Maxwell would have been amazed if he could have measured the extent of desire on the part of his people to take up the cross.

The service was over, the great audience had gone, and Maxwell again faced the company gathered in the lecture room as on the two previous Sundays. The after-service seemed now to be a necessity. As he went in and faced the people, his heart trembled. There were at least one hundred present. The Holy Spirit was never before so manifest. He missed Jasper Chase. But all the others were present.

Chapter 11

"Your sermon today made clear to me what I have long been feeling I ought to do," Donald Marsh, president of Lincoln College, said as he and Mr. Maxwell walked home. " 'What would Jesus do in my place?' I've asked the question repeatedly since I made my promise. I've tried to satisfy myself that He would simply go on as I have done, attending to the duties of my college work, teaching my classes. But I've been able to avoid the feeling that He would do something more. Something I don't want to do, as it will cause me genuine suffering to do it. I dread it with all my soul. But I shall never be satisfied until I carry this cross."

"Yes, I think I know. It is my cross, too. I would almost rather do anything else."

Donald Marsh looked surprised, then relieved. "Maxwell, we've lived in a little world of literature and scholarly seclusion, doing work we have enjoyed and shrinking from the disagreeable duties of citizenship. Our city officials are a corrupt, unprincipled set of men, controlled in large part by the whiskey element and thoroughly selfish so far as the affairs of city government are concerned. Yet I've been satisfied to let them run the municipality and have lived in my little world, out of touch and sympathy with the real world of the people. 'What would Jesus do?' I have even tried to avoid an honest answer. But my plain duty is to take a personal part in this coming election, go to the primaries, throw the weight of my influence, whatever it is, toward the nomination and election of good men, and plunge into the very depths of the entire horrible whirlpool of deceit, bribery, political trickery, and saloonism as it exists in Raymond today."

"You have spoken for me also," replied Maxwell with a sad smile. "All my parish work, all my little trials or self-sacrifices, are as nothing to me compared with the breaking into my scholarly, intellectual, self-contained habits of this open, coarse, public fight for a clean city life. The answer to the question, 'What would Jesus do?' in this case leaves me no peace except when I say Jesus would have me act the part of a Christian citizen. We can do no less than take up this cross and follow Him."

The two men then walked on in silence for a while. Finally, President Marsh said, "We do not need to act alone in this matter. With all the men who have made the promise, we certainly can have companionship and strength, even, of numbers. Let us organize the Christian forces of Raymond for the battle against rum and corruption, a campaign that will mean something because it is organized righteousness. Jesus would use great wisdom in this matter. He would employ means. He would make large plans. Let us do so."

They talked over the matter a long time and met again the next day in Maxwell's study to develop plans. The city primaries were called for Friday, a public meeting at the courthouse.

In its Saturday edition the evening *News* gave a full account of the primaries, and in the editorial columns Edward Norman spoke with a directness and conviction that the Christian people of Raymond were learning to respect.

> *Never before in the history of Raymond was there a primary like the one in the courthouse last night. It was a complete surprise to the city of politicians who have been in the habit of carrying on the affairs of the city as if they owned them. A large number of the citizens of Raymond who have never before taken part in the city's affairs entered the primary and controlled it, nominating some of the best men for all the offices to be filled at the coming election.*
>
> *It was a tremendous lesson in good citizenship. President Marsh of Lincoln College made one of the best speeches ever made in Raymond. The consternation deepened as the primary proceeded and it became*

evident that the old-time ring of city rulers was outnumbered.

Scores of well-known businessmen and professional men, most of them church members, were present, and it did not take long to see that they had all come with the one direct and definite purpose of nominating the best men possible. Most of those men had never before been seen in a primary. They were complete strangers to the politicians. But they were able by organized and united effort to nominate the entire ticket.

As soon as it became plain that the primary was out of their control, the regular ring withdrew in disgust and nominated another ticket. The News simply calls the attention of all decent citizens to the fact that the line is sharply and distinctly drawn between the saloon and corrupt management, such as we have known for years, and a clean, honest, capable, businesslike city administration, such as every good citizen ought to want.

The crisis of our city affairs has been reached. The issue is squarely before us. Shall we continue the rule of rum and bribery and shameless incompetence, or shall we, as President Marsh said in his noble speech, rise as good citizens and begin a new order of things, cleansing our city of the worst enemy known to municipal honesty, and doing what lies in our power to do with the ballot to purify our civic life?

For the first time in its history, Raymond had seen the professional men—the teachers, the college professors, the doctors, the ministers—take political action and put themselves definitely in public antagonism to the evil forces that had so long controlled the machine of the municipal government.

❖

Saturday afternoon as Virginia stepped out of her house to go and see Rachel, a carriage drove up containing three of her fashionable friends. They wanted Virginia to go driving with them up on the boulevard. The day was too pleasant to be spent indoors.

"Where have you been all this time, Virginia?" asked one of the girls, tapping her playfully on the shoulder with a red silk parasol. "We hear that you have gone into the show business. Tell us about it."

Virginia colored, but she frankly told something of her experience at the Rectangle.

"I tell you, girls, let's go 'slumming' with Virginia this afternoon. I've never been down to the Rectangle. I've heard it's an awful, wicked place and lots to see. Virginia will act as guide, and it will be interesting."

The other girls seemed to be of the same mind with the speaker, and Virginia suddenly saw an opportunity. These girls had never seen the sin and misery of Raymond. Why should they not see it, even if their motive in going down there was simply to pass away an afternoon?

"Very well, I'll go with you, but you must let me take you where you can see the most," she said as she entered the carriage.

Chapter 12

"Hadn't we better take a policeman along?" said one of the girls with a nervous laugh.

"There's no danger," said Virginia briefly.

"Is it true that your brother, Rollin, converted?" asked another.

It struck Virginia that all three of her friends were regarding her with close attention as if she were peculiar. "Yes, he certainly is."

"I understand he's going around to the clubs talking with his old friends there, trying to preach to them," said the girl with the red silk parasol.

Virginia did not answer, and as they neared the district, the girls grew more and more nervous. As they entered farther into the district, the Rectangle seemed to stare as with one great, bleary, beer-soaked countenance at this fine carriage with its load of fashionably dressed young women. Frightened and disgusted, the girls felt that instead of seeing the Rectangle, they were the objects of curiosity.

"Let's go back," said the girl sitting with Virginia.

At that moment they were just opposite a notorious saloon and gambling house. The street was narrow and the sidewalk crowded. Suddenly, out of the door of this saloon a young woman reeled. She sang in a broken, drunken sob that indicated she partly realized her awful condition—"Just as I am, without one plea"—and as the carriage rolled past, she leered at it. Virginia recognized the face of the girl who had knelt sobbing the night Virginia knelt beside her, praying for her.

"Stop!" cried Virginia. The carriage stopped, and in a moment she was out and took the girl by the arm. "Loreen!"

The girl looked into her face, and her own changed into a look of utter horror. The saloonkeeper came to the door of the saloon and stood there looking on with his hands on his hips. And the Rectangle, from its windows, its saloon steps, its filthy sidewalk, gutter, and roadway, paused and with undisguised wonder stared at the two girls. Over the scene the warm sun of spring poured its mellow light.

Virginia simply saw a soul that had tasted of the joy of a better life slipping back again into its old hell of shame and death. She asked only one question, "What would Jesus do?" She looked around now as she stood with Loreen, and the whole scene was cruelly vivid to her.

"Drive on; don't wait for me. I am going to see my friend home," she said calmly to the girls in the carriage.

The girl with the red parasol gasped at the word *friend*, but she didn't say anything. The other girls were speechless.

The carriage moved on, and Virginia was alone with her charge. She looked up and around. Many faces in the crowd were sympathetic. The Holy Spirit had softened a good deal of the Rectangle.

"Where does she live?" asked Virginia.

No one answered.

The girl suddenly wrenched her arm from Virginia's grasp, nearly throwing Virginia down. "Leave me! Let me go to hell! That's where I belong!" she exclaimed hoarsely.

Virginia stepped up to her and put her arm about her. "Loreen," she said firmly, "come with me. You do not belong to hell. You belong to Jesus and He will save you. Come."

The girl suddenly burst into tears.

Virginia looked around again. "Where does Mr. Gray live?" she asked. A number of voices gave the address.

"Come, Loreen. Go with me to Mr. Gray's," she said, still keeping her hold of the swaying, trembling creature, who moaned and sobbed and now clung to her.

So the two moved on through the Rectangle toward the

evangelist's lodging place. The sight seemed to impress the Rectangle seriously. The fact that one of the richest, most beautifully dressed girls in all Raymond was taking care of one of the Rectangle's most noted characters, who reeled along under the influence of liquor, was a fact astounding enough to throw dignity and importance about Loreen herself. When they finally reached Mr. Gray's lodging place, the woman who answered Virginia's knock said that both Mr. and Mrs. Gray were out somewhere and would not be back until six o'clock.

Virginia had not planned anything further than a possible appeal to the Grays, either to take charge of Loreen for a while or to find some safe place for her until she was sober. She stood now at the door, at a loss to know what to do. Finally, a thought possessed her that she could not escape. What was to hinder her from taking Loreen home with her? Why should not this homeless, wretched creature, reeking with the fumes of liquor, be cared for in Virginia's own home instead of being consigned to strangers in some hospital or house of charity? "Loreen, come. You are going home with me."

Loreen staggered to her feet and, to Virginia's surprise, made no trouble. She had expected resistance or a stubborn refusal to move. When they reached the corner and took the car, it was nearly full of people going uptown. Virginia was painfully conscious of the stare that greeted her and her companion as they entered. Loreen was lapsing into a state of stupor, and Virginia was obliged to hold fast to her arm. Several times the girl lurched heavily against her. When she mounted the steps of her handsome house, Virginia breathed a sigh of relief, even in the face of the interview with her grandmother, and when the door shut and she was in the wide hall with her homeless outcast, she felt equal to anything that might come.

Hearing Virginia come in, Madam Page came into the hall. Virginia stood there supporting Loreen, who stared stupidly at the rich magnificence of the furnishings around her.

"Grandmother"—Virginia spoke without hesitation and very clearly—"I have brought one of my friends from the Rectangle.

She is in trouble and has no home. I am going to care for her here a little while."

Madam Page glanced from her granddaughter to Loreen in astonishment.

"Did you say she is one of your friends?" she asked in a cold, sneering voice.

"Yes." Virginia's face flushed, but she recalled a verse that Mr. Gray had used for one of his recent sermons, "A friend of publicans and sinners." Surely Jesus would do this that she was doing.

"Do you know what this girl is?" asked Madam Page in an angry whisper, stepping near Virginia.

"I know very well. She is an outcast. I know it even better than you do. She is drunk at this minute. But she is also a child of God. I have seen her on her knees, repentant. And I have seen hell reach out its horrible fingers after her again. And by the grace of Christ, I feel that the least I can do is to rescue her from such peril."

Madam Page glared at Virginia and clenched her hands. All this was contrary to her social code of conduct. What would Virginia's action cost the family in the way of criticism and loss of standing? To Madam Page society represented more than the church or any other institution. It was a power to be feared and obeyed. She stood erect and stern and confronted Virginia, fully roused and determined. Virginia placed her arm about Loreen and calmly looked her grandmother in the face.

"You shall not do this, Virginia! You can send her to the asylum for helpless women. We can pay all the expenses. We cannot afford, for the sake of our reputations, to shelter such a person."

"Grandmother, I do not wish to do anything that is displeasing to you, but I must keep Loreen here tonight, and longer if it seems best."

"Then you can answer for the consequences! I do not stay in the same house with a miserable—" Madam Page lost her self-control.

Virginia stopped her before she could speak the next word. "Grandmother, this house is mine. It is your home as long as you choose to remain. But in this matter I must act as I fully believe

Jesus would in my place."

"I shall not stay here, then!" said Madam Page. "You can always remember that you have driven your grandmother out of your house in favor of a drunken woman." Then, without waiting for Virginia to reply, she turned and went upstairs.

Virginia called a servant and soon had Loreen cared for.

Chapter 13

When the bell rang for tea, Virginia went down, but her grandmother did not appear. A few minutes later Rollin came in. He brought word that his grandmother had taken the evening train for the South. He had been at the station to see some friends off and had by chance met his grandmother as he was coming out. She had told him her reason for going.

"Rollin," said Virginia, "am I wrong?"

"No, dear, I cannot believe you are. If you think this poor creature owes her safety and salvation to your personal care, it was the only thing for you to do. Surely Jesus in our places would do what you have done."

Of all the wonderful changes that Virginia was to know on account of her great pledge, nothing affected her so powerfully as the thought of Rollin's change of life. Truly, this man in Christ was a new creature.

Dr. West came that evening at Virginia's summons and did everything necessary for the outcast. The best that could be done for her now was quiet nursing and careful watching and personal love.

❖

The after-meeting at the First Church was now eagerly established. Henry Maxwell went into the lecture room on the Sunday succeeding the week of the primary and noted again the absence of Jasper Chase. All the others were present, and they were drawn together by a bond of common fellowship that demanded and enjoyed mutual confidences.

In the spirit of very open, frank confession of experience, it seemed the most natural thing in the world for Edward Norman to tell all the rest of the company about the details of his newspaper.

"I have lost a great deal of money during the last three weeks. I am losing a great many subscribers every day."

"What do the subscribers give as their reason for dropping the paper?" asked Mr. Maxwell. All the rest listened eagerly.

"There are a good many different reasons. Some say they want a paper that prints all the crime details, sensations like prizefights, scandals, and horrors of various kinds. Others object to the discontinuance of the Sunday edition. My greatest loss has come from a falling off in advertisements and from the attitude I have taken on political questions. I may as well tell you all frankly that if I continue to pursue the plan which I honestly believe Jesus would pursue in the matter of political issues and their treatment from a nonpartisan and moral standpoint, the *News* will not be able to pay its operating expenses."

He paused a moment, and the room was very quiet.

He went on. "Are there enough genuine Christian people in Raymond who will rally to the support of a paper such as Jesus would probably edit? Or are the habits of the church people so firmly established in their demand for the regular type of journalism that they will not take a paper unless it is stripped largely of the Christian and moral purpose? I may say in this fellowship gathering that owing to recent complications in my business affairs outside of my paper, I have lost a large part of my fortune. It is not necessary for me to go into details. I mention it because I have the fullest faith in the final success of a daily paper conducted on the lines I have recently laid down, and I had planned to put into it my entire fortune in order to win final success. As it is now, unless the Christian people of Raymond—the church members and professing disciples—will support the paper with subscriptions and advertisements, I cannot continue its publication on the present basis."

Virginia followed Mr. Norman's confession with the most intense eagerness. She now asked, "Do you mean that a Christian daily ought to be endowed with a large sum like a Christian college in order to make it pay?"

"That is exactly what I mean. I've laid out plans for putting into the *News* a variety of material in a strong and truly interesting way that it would more than make up for whatever was absent from its columns in the way of unchristian matter. I'm very confident that a Christian daily such as Jesus would approve can be made to succeed financially. But it will take a large sum of money to work out the plans."

"How much, do you think?" asked Virginia quietly.

Edward Norman looked at her keenly. "I should say half a million dollars in a town like Raymond could be well spent in the establishment of a paper such as we have in mind," he answered. His voice trembled a little.

"Then," said Virginia, speaking as if the thought was fully considered, "I am ready to put that amount of money into the paper on the one condition, of course, that it be carried on as it has been begun."

"Thank God!" exclaimed Mr. Maxwell softly. Norman was pale.

Virginia went on, "I have come to know that the money, which I have called my own, is not mine but God's. If I, as a steward of His, see some wise way to invest His money, it is not an occasion for vainglory or thanks from anyone simply because I have proved honest in my administration of the funds He has asked me to use for His glory. I've been thinking of this very plan for some time. The fact is, we need the *News* to champion the Christian side. It would be giving up to the enemy to allow the *News* to fail. I have great confidence in Mr. Norman's ability. If we can keep such a paper going for one year, I shall be willing to see that amount of money used in the experiment. I believe it is what Jesus would do."

No one spoke for a while. Mr. Maxwell, standing there where the faces lifted their intense gaze into his, felt what he had already felt—a strange movement out of the nineteenth century into the first, when the disciples had all things in common and a spirit of fellowship must have flowed freely between them such as the First

Church of Raymond had never before known. It had the effect that a physical miracle may have had on the early disciples in giving them a feeling of confidence in the Lord that helped them to face loss and martyrdom with courage and even joy.

Chapter 14

Election week followed this Sunday meeting. President Marsh, true to his promise, tore himself out of the scholarly seclusion of years with a pain and anguish that cost him more than anything he had ever done as a follower of Christ. With him were a few of the college professors who had made the pledge in the First Church. Henry Maxwell also plunged into the horror of this fight against whiskey and its allies with a sickening dread of each day's new encounter with it. He staggered under it, and in the brief intervals when he came in from the work and sought the quiet of his study for rest, the sweat broke out on his forehead, and he felt the actual terror of one who marches into unseen, unknown horrors. When Saturday, the election day, came, the excitement rose to its height. An attempt to close all the saloons was only partly successful. The Rectangle boiled and heaved and cursed and turned its worst side out to the gaze of the city.

Gray continued his meetings during the week, and the results had been even greater than he had dared to hope. When Saturday came, it seemed to him that the crisis in his work had been reached. The Holy Spirit and the Satan of rum rose up in a desperate conflict. The saloon men no longer concealed their feelings, making open threats of violence. Once during the week, Gray and his little company of helpers were assailed with missiles of various kinds as they left the tent late at night. Rachel's power in song had not diminished. Rather, with each night, it seemed to add to the intensity and reality of the Spirit's presence.

Gray had at first hesitated about having a meeting that Saturday night. But the Spirit seemed to lead him to continue the meeting, and so Saturday night he went on as usual.

The excitement all over the city reached its climax when the polls closed at six o'clock. Never before had there been such a contest in Raymond. Never before had such elements in the city been arrayed against each other. It was an unheard-of thing that the president of Lincoln College, the pastor of the First Church, the dean of the Cathedral, the professional men living in fine houses on the boulevard, should come personally into the wards and by their presence and their example represent the Christian conscience of the place. The fight grew hotter every hour, and when six o'clock came neither side could have guessed at the result with any certainty. Both sides awaited the announcement of the result with the greatest interest.

It was after ten o'clock when the meeting at the tent closed. Maxwell had come down again at Gray's request. He was completely worn-out by the day's work, but the appeal from Gray came to him in such a form that he did not feel able to resist it. President Marsh was also present. He had never been to the Rectangle, and his curiosity was aroused. Dr. West and Rollin had come with Rachel and Virginia; and Loreen, who still stayed with Virginia, was present near the organ, in her right mind, sober, with a humility and dread of herself that kept her as close to Virginia as a faithful dog. The returns from the election were beginning to come in, and the Rectangle had emptied every lodging house, den, and hovel into the streets. Once in a while a shout from the large crowd swept into the tent.

In spite of these distractions, Rachel's singing kept the crowd in the tent from dissolving. There were a dozen or more conversions. Finally, the people became restless and Gray closed the service, remaining a little while with the converts.

Rachel, Virginia, Loreen, Rollin, President Marsh, Mr. Maxwell, and Dr. West went out together, intending to go down to the usual waiting place for their car. Outside the tent, they were at once aware that the Rectangle trembled on the verge of a drunken riot, and as they pushed through the gathering mobs in the narrow streets, they realized that they themselves were objects of great attention.

"There he is—the bloke in the tall hat! He's the leader!" shouted a rough voice. President Marsh, with his erect, commanding figure, was conspicuous in the little company.

"How has the election gone? It is too early to know the result yet, isn't it?" He asked the question aloud, and a man answered.

"They say second and third wards have gone almost solid for no-license. If that is so, the whiskey men have been beaten."

"Thank God! I hope it is true!" exclaimed Maxwell. "Marsh, we are in danger here. We ought to get the ladies to a place of safety."

At that moment a shower of stone and other missiles fell over them. The narrow street and sidewalk in front of them was completely choked with the worst elements of the Rectangle.

"This looks serious," said Maxwell. With Marsh and Rollin and Dr. West, he started to go forward through a small opening. Virginia, Rachel, and Loreen followed closely sheltered by the men. "Down with the aristocrats!" shouted a shrill voice, more like a woman's than a man's. A shower of mud and stones followed. Rachel remembered afterward that Rollin jumped directly in front of her and received on his head and chest a number of blows that probably would have struck her if he had not shielded her from them.

Then Loreen darted forward in front of Virginia and pushed her aside, looking up and screaming. It was so sudden that no one had time to catch the face of the one who did it. But out of the upper window of a room, over the very saloon where Loreen had come out a week before, someone threw a heavy bottle. It struck Loreen on the head, and she fell to the ground. Virginia turned and instantly knelt down by her. President Marsh raised his arm and shouted over the howl that was beginning to rise from the wild beast in the mob.

"Stop! You've killed a woman!" The announcement partly sobered the crowd.

"Is it true?" Maxwell asked as Dr. West knelt on the other side of Loreen, supporting her.

"She's dying!" said Dr. West briefly.

Loreen opened her eyes and smiled at Virginia, who wiped the blood from her face and then bent over and kissed her. Loreen smiled again, and the next minute her soul was in paradise.

Chapter 15

Sunday morning Loreen's body lay in state at the Page mansion on the avenue. The clear, sweet spring air swept over the casket from one of the open windows at the end of the grand hall. Church bells rang, and people on the avenue service turned curious, inquiring looks up at the great house and then went on.

At the First Church, Mr. Maxwell, bearing on his face marks of the scene he had been through, confronted an immense congregation and spoke to it with a passion and a power that came naturally out of the profound experiences of the day before. All through his impassioned appeal this morning, there was a note of sadness and rebuke and stern condemnation that made many of the members pale with self-accusation or with inward anger.

Raymond had awakened that morning to the fact that the city had gone for license after all. A meager majority won the victory, it was true, but the result was the same as if it had been overwhelming. The Christians of Raymond stood condemned by the result. More than a hundred professing Christian disciples had failed to go to the polls, and many more than that number had voted with the whiskey men.

With a voice that rang and trembled and broke in sobs of anguish for the result, Henry Maxwell poured out upon his people these truths that Sunday morning. And men and women wept as he spoke. President Marsh sat there, his usual erect, handsome, firm, bright, self-confident bearing all gone; his head bowed upon his breast, the great tears rolling down his cheeks, unmindful of the fact that never before had he shown outward emotion in a public service. Edward Norman sat nearby with his clear-cut, keen face erect, but his lip trembled, and he clutched the end of the pew with a feeling of emotion that struck deep into his knowledge of the truth as Maxwell spoke it. The thought that the Christian conscience had been aroused too late or too feebly lay with a weight of accusation upon the heart of the editor. And up in the choir, Rachel Winslow, with her face bowed on the railing of the oak screen, gave way to a feeling that she had not allowed yet to master her, but it so unfitted her for her part that when Mr. Maxwell finished and she tried to sing the closing solo after the prayer, her voice broke, and for the first time in her life, she was obliged to sit down, sobbing and unable to go on.

When the congregation had finally gone and Maxwell entered the lecture room, it needed but a glance to show him that the original company of followers had been largely increased. The meeting was tender; it glowed with the Spirit's presence; it was alive with strong and lasting resolve to begin a war on the whiskey power in Raymond that would break its reign forever. It was a meeting full of broken prayers of contrition, of confession, of strong yearning for a new and better city life.

The Rectangle also felt moved strangely in its own way. Loreen's death was not in itself so remarkable a fact. It was her recent acquaintance with the people from the city that lifted her into special prominence and surrounded her death with more than ordinary importance. Everyone in the Rectangle knew that Loreen was at this moment lying in the Page mansion up on the avenue. Inquirers besieged Gray and his wife, wanting to know what Loreen's friends and acquaintances were expected to do in paying their last respects to her.

So that is how it happened that Monday afternoon Loreen's funeral service was held at the tent before an immense audience that choked the tent and overflowed beyond all previous bounds.

Virginia with her uncle and Rollin, accompanied by Maxwell, Rachel, President Marsh, and the quartet from the First Church, went down and witnessed one of the strangest things of their lives.

A somewhat noted newspaper correspondent passed through Raymond that afternoon. He heard of the service at the tent and went down. His description caught the attention of very many readers the next day.

A very unique and unusual funeral service was held in the slum district known as the Rectangle this afternoon at the tent of an evangelist, Reverend John Gray. The woman, killed during an election riot last Saturday night, had been recently converted during the evangelist's meetings. She was a common street drunkard, and yet the services at the tent were as impressive as any I ever witnessed in a metropolitan church over the most distinguished citizen.

A trained choir sang a most exquisite anthem. But the most remarkable part of the music was a solo sung by a strikingly beautiful young woman, a Miss Winslow. She had a most wonderful manner in singing, and everybody was weeping before she had sung a dozen words. That, of course, is not so strange an effect to be produced at a funeral service, but the voice itself was one of thousands. Miss Winslow sings in the First Church of Raymond and could probably command almost any salary as a public singer.

The service was peculiar. The evangelist, a man of apparently very simple, unassuming style, spoke a few words, and he was followed by a fine-looking man, the Reverend Henry Maxwell, pastor of the First Church of Raymond. He spoke in a peculiarly sensitive manner of the effect of the liquor business on the lives of men and women like this one. Raymond is full of saloons. I caught from the minister's remarks that only recently he had changed his views in regard to license. He certainly made a very striking address, and yet it was in no sense inappropriate for a funeral.

Then followed what was perhaps the oddest part of this strange service. The women in the tent, many of them up near the coffin, began to sing in a soft, tearful way, "I was a wandering sheep." Then while the singing was going on, one row of women stood up and walked slowly past the casket, and as they went by, each one placed a flower of some kind upon it. Then they sat down and another row filed past, leaving their flowers. All the time the singing continued softly like rain on a tent cover when the wind is gentle. It was one of the simplest and at the same time one of the most impressive sights I ever witnessed. There must have been a hundred of these women, and I was told many of them had been converted at the meetings just recently. I cannot describe the effect of that singing. All women's voices, and so soft, and yet so distinct, that the effect was startling.

The service closed with another solo by Miss Winslow, who sang, "There were ninety and nine." And then the evangelist asked them all to bow their heads while he prayed. The last view I caught of the service was of the great crowd pouring out of the tent and forming in open ranks while the coffin was borne out by six of the women. It is a long time since I have seen such a picture in this unpoetic republic.

Chapter 16

No one in all Raymond, including the Rectangle, felt Loreen's death more keenly than Virginia. That short week while the girl had been in her home had opened Virginia's heart to a new life. The day after the funeral, Rachel called on Virginia, and they sat in the hall of the Page mansion.

Virginia looked over to the end of the hall where Loreen's body had lain. "I've decided on a good plan, as it seems to me. After talking to Rollin, he and I will devote a large part of our money to help those women to a better life.

"Rachel, I want you to work with me. Rollin and I are going to buy up a large part of the property in the Rectangle. The field where the tent now is has been in litigation for years. We mean to secure the entire tract as soon as the courts have settled the title. The money God wants me to use can build wholesome lodging-homes, refuges for poor women, asylums for shop girls, safety for many a lost girl like Loreen. But I don't want to simply dispense the money. I want to put myself into the problem." Virginia suddenly rose and paced the hall. "However, all that limitless money and limitless personal sacrifice can possibly do will not really lessen very much the awful condition at the Rectangle as long as the saloon is legally established there."

Rachel answered with a note of hope in her voice. "It is true. But, Virginia, what a wonderful amount of good can be done with this money! And the saloon cannot always remain here. The time must come when the Christian forces in the city will triumph."

Virginia paused near Rachel, and her pale, earnest face lit up. "The number of those who have promised to do as Jesus would is increasing. If we ever have, say, five hundred such disciples in Raymond, the saloon is doomed. But now, dear, I want you to look at your part in this plan for capturing and saving the Rectangle. You could organize among the girls a musical institute, give them the benefit of your voice training. Did anyone ever hear such singing as that yesterday by those women? You shall have the best of material in the way of organs and orchestras that money can provide. Much can be done with music to win souls into higher and purer and better living."

The thought of her lifework flowed into Rachel's heart and mind like a flood, and the torrent of her feeling overflowed in tears that could not be restrained. It was what she had dreamed of doing. "Yes," she said as she rose and put her arm about Virginia. "Yes, I will gladly put my life into that kind of service." Both girls now paced the hall with enthusiasm.

"Add to the money consecrated personal enthusiasm like yours, and it certainly can accomplish great things," said Virginia, smiling.

Before Rachel could reply, Rollin came in. He hesitated a moment. Then, as he passed out of the hall into the library, Virginia called him back and asked him some questions about his work.

Rollin came back and sat down, and together the three discussed their future plans. Rollin, apparently free from embarrassment in Rachel's presence while Virginia was with them, still treated her with a politeness that was almost cold. He had not forgotten the past, but he was completely caught up for this present time in the purpose of his new life. After a while Rollin was called out, and the girls talked of other things.

"By the way, what has become of Jasper Chase?" Virginia asked the question innocently, but Rachel flushed, and Virginia added with a smile, "I suppose he is writing another book. Is he going to put you into this one, Rachel? You know I always suspected him of doing that very thing in his first story."

"Jasper told me the other night that he—in fact—he proposed

to me—or he would, if—" Rachel stopped and sat with her hands clasped on her lap. There were tears in her eyes. "I thought not long ago I loved him, as he said he loved me. But when he spoke, my heart felt repelled, and I told him no. I have not seen him since."

"I am glad for you," said Virginia quietly.

"Why?" asked Rachel, a little startled.

"Because he is too cold and—I do not like to judge him, but I have always distrusted his sincerity in taking the pledge at the church with the rest."

Rachel looked at Virginia thoughtfully.

"I have never given my heart to him, I am sure. I think perhaps if he had spoken to me at any other time than the one he chose, I could easily have persuaded myself that I loved him. But not now."

After Rachel left, Virginia sat in the hall thinking over the confidence her friend had just shown her. Soon Rollin came back, and he and Virginia walked arm in arm up and down the long hall. It was easy for their talk to settle finally upon Rachel because of the place she occupied in their plans for the Rectangle.

"Did you ever know of a girl of such really gifted powers in vocal music who was willing to give her life to the people as Rachel is going to do?"

"It is certainly a very good example of self-sacrifice," replied Rollin a little stiffly.

Virginia looked at him a little sharply but said nothing. The two walked on in silence for the length of the hall.

Then Virginia spoke: "Rollin, why do you treat Rachel with such a distinct, precise manner? I think that she is annoyed by it. You need to be on easy terms."

Rollin suddenly stopped, deeply agitated. He took his arm from Virginia's and walked alone to the end of the hall. Then he returned, with his hands behind him, and stopped near his sister. "Virginia, have you not learned my secret?"

Virginia looked bewildered; then over her face the unusual color crept, showing that she understood.

"I have never loved anyone but Rachel Winslow." Rollin spoke calmly enough now. "That day she was here when you talked about her refusal to join the concert company, I asked her to be my wife. She refused me, and she gave as her reason the fact I had no purpose in life, which was true enough. Now that I have a purpose, now that I am a new man, it's impossible for me to say anything. I owe my very conversion to Rachel's singing. And yet that night while she sang, I can honestly say that for the time being, I never thought of her voice except as God's message." Rollin was silent; then he went on with more emotion. "I still love her, Virginia. But I do not think she ever could love me." He stopped and looked at his sister with a sad smile.

Virginia noted Rollin's handsome face, his marks of dissipation nearly all gone now, the firm lips showing manhood and courage, the clear eyes looking into hers frankly, the form strong and graceful. Rollin was a man now. Why shouldn't Rachel come to love him in time? Surely the two were well fitted for each other, especially now that the same Christian force motivated their purpose in life.

Chapter 17

The next day Virginia went down to the *News* office to see Edward Norman and Mr. Maxwell and arrange the details of her part in the establishment of the paper on its new foundation.

"I have written down some of the things that it has seemed to me Jesus would do," said Edward Norman. He read from a paper lying on his desk.

"I have headed this 'What would Jesus do as editor of a daily newspaper in Raymond?'

"1. He would never allow anything in His paper that could be called bad or coarse or impure.

"2. He would conduct the political part of the paper from the standpoint of the advancement of the kingdom of God on earth."

Edward Norman looked up from the reading a moment. "You understand that I am simply trying to answer honestly.

"3. Jesus' aim of a daily paper would be to do the will of God, not to make money or gain political influence.

"4. All questionable advertisements would be impossible.

"5. Jesus' relations to the employees on the paper would be of the most loving character.

"So far as I have gone," said Norman, again looking up, "I am of the opinion that Jesus would use some form of cooperation that represented the idea of a mutual interest in a business where all worked together for the same great end, and expressed not only in personal love and sympathy for the other employees but also in a sharing of the profits of the business.

"6. Jesus would give large space to the work of the Christian world—devoting space to the facts of reform, sociological problems, institutional church work, and similar movements.

"7. He would do all in His power in His paper to fight the saloon as an enemy of the human race and an unnecessary part of our civilization, regardless of public sentiment and regardless of its effect upon His subscription list."

Again Edward Norman looked up. "I state my honest conviction on this point. I believe He would use the influence of His paper to remove the saloon entirely from the political and social life of the nation.

"8. Jesus would not issue a Sunday edition.

"9. He would print the news of the world that people ought to know, but nothing which in any way would conflict with the first point in this outline.

"10. Jesus would secure the best and strongest Christian men and women to cooperate with Him in the matter of contributions.

"11. The main principle that guides the paper is the establishment of the kingdom of God in the world. This large general principle would necessarily shape all the detail.

"This is merely a faint outline. I have a hundred ideas for making the paper powerful that I have not thought out fully as yet. As I have talked it over with other newspapermen, some of them say I will have a weak, namby-pamby Sunday school sheet. If I get out something as good as a Sunday school, it will be pretty good. But the paper will not necessarily be weak because it is good. Good things are more powerful than bad. The question with me is largely one of support from the Christian people of Raymond. There are over twenty thousand church members here in this city. If half of them will stand by the *News*, its life is assured. What do you think, Maxwell, of the probability of such support?"

"I don't know enough about it to give an intelligent answer. The great thing will be to issue such a paper, as near as we can judge, as Jesus probably would. Put into it all the elements of Christian brains, strength, intelligence, and sense, and command respect for freedom from bigotry, fanaticism, narrowness, and anything else that is contrary to the spirit of Jesus."

"Yes." Edward Norman spoke humbly. "I shall make a great many mistakes, no doubt. I need a great deal of wisdom. So I shall continue to ask the question and abide by the results."

"I think we are beginning to understand," said Virginia, "the meaning of that command, 'Grow in the grace and knowledge of our Lord and Savior Jesus Christ.' I am sure I do not know all that He would do in detail until I know Him better."

"That is very true," said Henry Maxwell. "I cannot interpret the probable action of Jesus until I know better what His Spirit is. The greatest question in all of human life is summed up when we ask, 'What would Jesus do?' if we also try to answer it from a growth in knowledge of Jesus Himself. We must know Jesus before we can imitate Him."

Virginia and Edward Norman worked out the details of their arrangement, and Norman found himself in possession of the sum of five hundred thousand dollars to use for the establishment of a Christian daily paper. When Virginia and Maxwell left, Norman closed his door and, alone with the Divine Presence, asked like a child for help from his all-powerful Father.

❀

Early one afternoon in August, after a day of refreshing coolness following a long period of heat, Jasper Chase walked to his window in the apartment house on the avenue and looked out.

On his desk lay a pile of manuscript. Since that evening when he had spoken to Rachel Winslow, he had not met her. His singularly sensitive nature served to thrust him into an isolation intensified by his habits as an author.

All through the heat of summer he wrote. His book was nearly done now. He threw himself into its construction with a feverish strength that threatened at any moment to desert him and leave him helpless.

He had not forgotten his pledge made with the other church

members at the First Church. It forced itself upon his notice all through his writing. "Would Jesus do this? Would He write this story?" It was a social novel, written in a style that had proved popular. It had no purpose except to amuse. Its moral teaching was not bad, but neither was it Christian in any positive way. Jasper Chase knew that such a story would probably sell. But he felt that Jesus would never write such a book.

The question obtruded on him at the most inopportune times. He became irascible over it. The standard of Jesus for an author was too ideal. Of course Jesus would use His powers to produce something useful or helpful, or with a purpose. But Jasper wrote for the same reason nearly every writer wrote for—money, money, and fame as a writer. He had no need to write for money. But his desire for fame urged him on. He must write this kind of matter. What would Jesus do? The question plagued him even more than Rachel's refusal.

As he stood at the window, Rollin Page came out of the clubhouse just opposite. Jasper noted his handsome face and noble figure as he started down the street. He went back to his desk and turned over some papers there, then came back to the window. Rollin now walked with Rachel Winslow. Rollin must have overtaken her as she was coming from Virginia's that afternoon.

Jasper watched the two figures until they disappeared in the crowd on the walk. Then he turned to his desk and began to write. When he had finished the last page of the last chapter of his book, it was nearly dark. "What would Jesus do?" He had finally answered the question by denying his Lord, deliberately choosing his course, urged on by his disappointment and loss.

Chapter 18

That afternoon when Rollin came upon Rachel Winslow as he turned into the avenue, his heart leaped up at the sight of her. He walked along by her now, rejoicing in a little moment of this earthly love he could not drive out of his life.

"Virginia tells me the arrangements are nearly completed for the transfer of the Rectangle property," Rachel said.

"Yes. It has been a tedious case in the courts. Did Virginia show you all the plans and specifications for building?"

"We looked over a good many. It is astonishing to me where Virginia has managed to get all her ideas about this work."

"Virginia knows more now about Arnold Toynbee and East End London and institutional church work in America than a good many professional slum workers." Rollin felt more at ease talking about the safe, common ground of their coming work of humanity. "What have you been doing all summer? I have not seen much of you," Rachel suddenly asked, and then her face warmed with its quick flush of tropical color.

"I've been busy," replied Rollin briefly.

"Tell me about it," persisted Rachel. "You say so little. Have I a right to ask?"

She put the question very frankly, turning toward Rollin in real earnest.

"Yes, certainly," he replied with a graceful smile. "I am not sure that I can tell you much. I've tried to find some way to reach the men I once knew and win them into more useful lives."

He stopped, almost afraid to go on, but Rachel kept quiet.

"I have made the pledge to do as I believe Jesus would do,"

continued Rollin, "and it is in trying to answer this question that I have been doing my work."

"It's wonderful to think that you are trying to keep that pledge. But what can you do with the clubmen?"

"That night at the tent," replied Rollin, his voice trembling a little, "I asked myself what purpose I could now have in my life to redeem it, to satisfy my thought of Christian discipleship. And the more I thought of it, the more I was driven to a place where I knew I must take up the cross. The churches look after the poor, miserable creatures like those in the Rectangle; they make some effort to reach working people; they have a large constituency among the average salary-earning people; they send money and missionaries to the foreign heathen. But the fashionable, dissipated young men around town, the clubmen, are left out of all plans for reaching and Christianizing. I know these men, their good and their bad qualities. I've been one of them. So that's what I have been trying to do, reach out to these men for Christ."

Rachel's interest in his plan was larger than mere curiosity. Rollin Page was so different now from the fashionable young man who had asked her to be his wife that she could not help thinking of him and talking with him as if he were an entirely new acquaintance.

They turned off the avenue and headed up the street to Rachel's home—the same street where Rollin had asked Rachel why she could not love him. They fell silent.

Rachel finally spoke. "In your work with your old acquaintances, what sort of reception do they give you? How do you approach them? What do they say?"

"It depends on the man. A good many of them think I am a crank. I've kept my membership up and am in good standing in that way. I try to be wise and not provoke any unnecessary criticism. Many of the men have responded to my appeal. Only a few nights ago a dozen men honestly and earnestly engaged in a conversation over religious matters. I've had the great joy of seeing some of the men give up bad habits and begin a new life. The men are not fighting shy of me, and I think that is a good sign. Also, I have actually interested some of them in the Rectangle work, and when it is started up, they will give something to help make it more powerful."

Rachel again noted the strong, manly tone of his speech as Rollin spoke with enthusiasm. With it all she knew there was a deep, underlying seriousness that felt the burden of the cross even while carrying it with joy. "Do you remember I reproached you once for not having any purpose worth living for?" she asked. "I want to say in justice to you now that I honor you for your courage and your obedience to the promise you have made as you interpret the promise. The life you are living is a noble one."

Rollin trembled, his agitation greater than he could control. Rachel could not help seeing it. At last he said, "I thank you. It is worth more to me than I can tell you to hear you say that." He looked into her face for one moment, noting that her face was more beautiful than ever.

She read his love for her in that look, but he did not speak.

When they separated, Rachel went into the house, and sitting down in her room, she put her face in her hands and said to herself: "I am beginning to know what it means to be loved by a noble man. I shall love Rollin Page after all."

She rose and walked back and forth, deeply moved. Nevertheless, it was evident to herself that her emotion was not that of regret or sorrow. A glad new joy had come to her. She rejoiced, for if she was beginning to love Rollin Page, it was the Christian man she had begun to love; the other never would have moved her to this great change.

Chapter 19

Letter from Rev. Calvin Bruce, DD, of the Nazareth Avenue Church, Chicago, to Rev. Philip A. Caxton, DD, New York City.

My dear Dr. Caxton,

It is late Sunday night, but I feel driven to write you now some account of the situation in Raymond as I have been studying it. It has apparently come to a climax today.

You remember Henry Maxwell in the seminary, a refined, scholarly fellow. When he was called to the First Church of Raymond within a year after leaving the seminary, I said to my wife, "Raymond has made a good choice. Maxwell will satisfy them as a sermonizer." He has been here eleven years, in a comfortable berth, with a very good salary, and pleasant surroundings, a not very exacting parish of refined, rich, respectable people.

A year ago today at the close of the service, Maxwell made the astounding proposition that the members of his church volunteer for a year not to do anything without first asking the question, "What would Jesus do?" and, after answering it, to do what in their honest judgment He would do, regardless of what the result might be to them.

The effect of this proposition has been so remarkable that the attention of the whole country has been directed to the movement. Maxwell tells me he was astonished at the response to his proposition. Some of the most prominent members in the church made the promise to do as Jesus would.

One needs to come here and learn something of the changes in individual lives, to realize all that is meant by this following of

Jesus' steps so literally. But I can give you some idea perhaps of what has been done as told me by friends here and by Maxwell himself.

The result of the pledge upon the First Church has been twofold. It has brought about a spirit of Christian fellowship, which Maxwell tells me impresses him as being very nearly what the Christian fellowship of the apostolic churches must have been; and it has divided the church into two distinct groups of members. Those who have not taken the pledge regard the others as foolishly literal in their attempt to imitate the example of Jesus. The effect on Maxwell is very marked. I heard him preach in our State Association four years ago. He impressed me at the time as having considerable power in dramatic delivery. His sermon was well written and abounded in what the seminary students used to call "fine passages."

This morning I heard Maxwell preach again. He is not the same man. He gives me the impression of one who has passed through a crisis of revolution. He tells me this revolution is simply a new definition of Christian discipleship.

He certainly has changed many of his old habits and many of his old views. The idea that is moving him on now is the idea that the Christianity of our times must represent a more literal imitation of Jesus, especially in the element of suffering. He seems filled with the conviction that what our churches need today, more than anything else, is this factor of joyful suffering for Jesus in some form.

I can give you some of the results on the individuals who have made this pledge and honestly tried to be true to it, so that you may see that this form of discipleship is not merely sentiment or fine posing for effect.

Take the case of Mr. Powers, who was superintendent of the machine shops of the L&T RR here. When he acted upon the evidence that incriminated the road, he lost his position, and his family and social relations have changed so that he and his family no longer appear in public. The president of the road, who was the principal offender, has resigned. Meanwhile, the superintendent has gone back to his old work as a telegraph operator. I met him at the church yesterday. He impressed me as a man who had, like Maxwell, gone through a crisis in character. Or take the case of Mr. Norman, editor of the Daily News. He risked his entire fortune in obedience to what he believed was Jesus' action and revolutionized his entire conduct of the paper at the risk of failure. To my mind it is one of the most interesting and remarkable papers ever printed in the United States. It is so far above the ordinary conception of a daily paper that I am amazed at the result. He tells me that more Christians in the city are reading the paper. He is very confident of its final success. Then there is Milton Wright, the merchant. He has so revolutionized his business that no man is more beloved today in Raymond. During the winter, while he was lying dangerously ill at his home, scores of clerks volunteered to watch and help in any way possible, and his return to his store was greeted with marked demonstrations. All this was brought about by the element of personal love introduced into the business. It is a fact, however, that while he has lost heavily in some directions, he has increased his business and is today respected and honored as one of the best and most successful merchants in Raymond.

And there is Miss Winslow. She has chosen to give her great talent to the poor of the city. Her plans include a Musical Institute where choruses and classes in vocal music shall be a feature. In connection with her friend Miss Page, she has planned a course in music which, if carried out, will certainly do much to lift up the lives of the people down there. Miss Winslow expects to be married this spring to a brother of Miss Page who was once a society leader and clubman, and who was converted in a tent where his wife-to-be took an active part in the service. President Marsh of Lincoln College is a graduate of my alma mater, and I knew him slightly when I was in the senior year. He has taken an active part in the recent municipal campaign, and his influence in the city is regarded as a very large factor in the coming election. He impressed me as having fought out some hard questions and as having taken up some real burdens that have caused, and still do cause, that suffering that does not eliminate, but does appear to intensify, a positive and practical joy.

Chapter 20

I want to tell you something of the meeting in the First Church today.

As I said, I heard Maxwell preach. His sermon this morning was as different from his sermon at the Association meeting four years ago as if it had been thought out and preached by someone living on another planet. I was profoundly touched. His text was "What is that to thee? Follow thou Me." It was a most unusually impressive appeal to the Christians of Raymond to obey Jesus' teachings and follow in His steps regardless of what others might do.

At the close of the service there was the usual after-meeting that has become a regular feature of the First Church. Into this meeting have come all those who made the pledge to do as Jesus would do, and the time is spent in mutual fellowship, confession, question as to what Jesus would do in special cases, and prayer that the one great guide of every disciple's conduct may be the Holy Spirit.

Maxwell asked me to come into this meeting. I have never felt the Spirit's presence so powerfully.

I asked questions. It is very evident that many of these disciples have repeatedly carried their obedience to Jesus to the extreme limit, regardless of financial loss. There is no lack of courage or consistency at this point.

It is also true that some of the businessmen who took the pledge have lost great sums of money in this imitation of Jesus and may have, like Alexander Powers, lost valuable positions owing to the impossibility of doing what they had been accustomed to do and at the same time what they felt Jesus would do in the same place. Those who still have means have helped those who have suffered in this way. In this respect these disciples have all things in common.

I never dreamed that such Christian fellowship could exist in this age of the world. I was almost skeptical as to the witness of my own senses. I still seem to be asking myself if this is the close of the nineteenth century in America.

But now, dear friend, I come to the real cause of this letter, the real heart of the whole question as the First Church of Raymond has forced it upon me. Before the meeting closed today, steps were taken to secure the cooperation of all other Christian disciples in this country. I think Maxwell took this step after long deliberation. The idea crystallized today in a plan to secure the fellowship of all the Christians in America. The churches, through their pastors, will be asked to form disciple gatherings like the one in the First Church. They will call for volunteers in the great body of church members in the United States, who will promise to do as Jesus would do.

Maxwell spoke particularly of the result of such general action on the saloon question. He is terribly in earnest over this. He told me that there was no question in his mind that the saloon would be beaten in Raymond at the election now near at hand. If so, they could go on with some courage to do the redemptive work begun by the evangelist and now taken up by the disciples in his own church. He convinced his church that the time had come for a fellowship with other Christians.

This is a grand idea, Caxton, but right here is where I find myself hesitating. I do not deny that the Christian disciple ought to follow Christ's steps as closely as these here in Raymond have tried to do. But I cannot avoid asking what the result would be if I ask my church in Chicago to do it.

I am writing this after feeling the solemn, profound touch of the Spirit's presence, and I confess to you, old friend, that I cannot call up in my church a dozen prominent business or professional men who would make this trial at the risk of all they hold dear.

The actual results of the pledge as obeyed here in Raymond are enough to make any pastor tremble, and at the same time long with yearning that they might occur in his own parish. Never have I seen a church so signally blessed by the Spirit as this one.

But—am I myself ready to take this pledge? I ask the question honestly, and I dread to face an honest answer. I know well enough that I should have to change very much in my life if I undertook to follow His steps so closely.

Shall I go back to my people next Sunday and stand up before them in my large city church and say, "Let us follow Jesus closer; let us walk in His steps where it will cost us something more than it is costing us now; let us pledge not to do anything without first asking: 'What would Jesus do?'"

If I should go before them with that message, it would be a strange and startling one to them. But why? Are we not ready to follow Him all the way? What is it to be a follower of Jesus? What does it mean to imitate Him? What does it mean to walk in His steps?

The Reverend Calvin Bruce, DD, of the Nazareth Avenue Church, Chicago, let his pen fall on the table. He had come to the parting of the ways, and his question, he felt sure, was the question of many and many a person in the ministry and in the church. He went to his window and opened it. Oppressed with the weight of his convictions, he felt almost suffocated with the air in the room. He wanted to see the stars and feel the breath of the world.

The night was very still. The clock in the First Church struck midnight. As it finished, a clear, strong voice down in the direction of the Rectangle came floating up to him as if borne on radiant pinions.

"Must Jesus bear the cross alone
And all the world go free?
No, there's a cross for everyone,
And there's a cross for me."

The Reverend Calvin Bruce turned away from the window, and after a little hesitation, he knelt. "What would Jesus do?" That was the burden of his prayer. Never had he yielded himself so completely to the Spirit of Jesus. He was on his knees a long time. He retired and slept fitfully with many awakenings. He rose before it was clear dawn and threw open his window again. As the light in the east grew stronger, he repeated to himself: "What would Jesus do? Shall I follow His steps?"

With this question throbbing through his whole being, Dr. Bruce went back to Chicago, and the great crisis in his Christian life in the ministry suddenly broke irresistibly upon him.

Chapter 21

The Saturday afternoon matinee at the Auditorium in Chicago was just over and the usual crowd struggled to get to its carriage before anyone else.

"Now then, 624," shouted the Auditorium attendant; "624!" he repeated, and there dashed up to the curb a splendid span of black horses attached to a carriage having the monogram "CRS" in gilt letters on the panel of the door.

Two girls stepped out of the crowd toward the carriage. The older one entered and took her seat, but the younger stood hesitating on the curb.

"Come, Felicia! What are you waiting for! I shall freeze to death!" called the voice from the carriage.

The girl outside of the carriage hastily unpinned a bunch of English violets from her dress and handed them to a small boy who stood shivering on the edge of the sidewalk almost under the horses' feet. He took them with a look of astonishment and a "Thank ye, lady!" and instantly buried a very grimy face in the bunch of perfume. The girl stepped into the carriage, the door shut with the incisive *bang*, and in a few moments the coachman was speeding the horses rapidly up one of the boulevards.

"You are always doing some peculiar thing or other, Felicia," said the older girl as the carriage whirled on past the great residences already brilliantly lighted.

"Am I? What have I done now, Rose?" asked the other.

"Oh, giving those violets to that boy! He looked as if he needed a good hot supper more than a bunch of violets. It's a wonder you didn't invite him home with us."

"Would it be peculiar to invite a boy like that to come to the house and get a hot supper?" Felicia asked the question softly.

"*Peculiar* isn't just the word, of course," replied Rose indifferently. "It would be what Madam Blanc calls 'outré.' Decidedly."

She yawned, and Felicia silently looked out of the window in the door.

"The concert was stupid and the violinist was simply a bore. I don't see how you could sit so still through it all," Rose exclaimed a little impatiently.

"I liked the music," answered Felicia quietly.

"You like anything. I never saw a girl with so little critical taste."

Felicia colored slightly but would not answer. Rose yawned again and then exclaimed abruptly, "I'm sick of 'most everything. I hope *The Shadows of London* will be exciting tonight. You know we have a box with the Delanos tonight."

Felicia turned her face toward her sister. Her great brown eyes were very expressive and not altogether free from a sparkle of luminous heat.

"And yet we never weep over the real thing on the actual stage of life. Why don't we get excited over the facts as they are?"

"Because the actual people are dirty and disagreeable and it's too much bother, I suppose," replied Rose carelessly. "Felicia, you can never reform the world. What's the use? We're not to blame for the poverty and misery."

"Suppose Christ had gone on that principle," replied Felicia with unusual persistence. "Do you remember Dr. Bruce's sermon on Second Corinthians 8:9 a few Sundays ago: 'For ye know the grace of our Lord Jesus Christ, that, though he was rich, yet for your sakes he became poor, that ye through his poverty might be rich'?"

"I remember it well enough," said Rose with some petulance, "and didn't Dr. Bruce go on to say that there is no blame attached to people who have wealth if they are kind and give to the needs of the poor? Ever since Rachel Winslow wrote about those strange doings in Raymond, you have upset the whole family. People can't live at that concert pitch all the time. You see if Rachel doesn't give it up soon. It's a great pity she doesn't come to Chicago and sing in the Auditorium concerts."

Felicia looked out of the window and was silent. The carriage rolled on past two blocks of magnificent private residences and turned into a wide driveway under a covered passage, and the sisters hurried into the house. It was an elegant mansion of gray stone furnished like a palace, every corner of it warm with the luxury of paintings, sculpture, art, and modern refinement.

The owner of it all, Mr. Charles R. Sterling, stood before an open grate fire smoking a cigar. He'd made his money in grain speculation and railroad ventures, and was reputed to be worth something over two million dollars. His wife, a sister of Mrs. Winslow of Raymond, had been an invalid for several years. The two girls, Rose and Felicia, were the only children.

Rose was twenty-one years old, fair, vivacious, educated in a fashionable college, just entering society and already somewhat cynical and indifferent. Felicia was nineteen, with a tropical beauty somewhat like that of her cousin Rachel, with warm, generous impulses just waking into Christian feeling, capable of all sorts of expression.

"Here's a letter for you, Felicia," said Mr. Sterling, handing it to her.

Felicia sat down and instantly opened the letter, saying as she did so, "It's from Rachel."

"Well, what's the latest news from Raymond?" asked Mr. Sterling, taking his cigar out of his mouth.

"Rachel says Dr. Bruce has been in Raymond for two Sundays and has seemed very interested in Mr. Maxwell's pledge in the First Church."

"What does Rachel say about herself?" asked Rose, who was lying on a couch almost buried under a half dozen elegant cushions.

"She is still singing at the Rectangle. Since the tent meetings closed, she sings in an old hall until the new buildings, which her friend Virginia Page is putting up, are completed."

Mr. Sterling lit a new cigar, and Rose exclaimed, "Rachel is so peculiar. She might set Chicago wild with her voice if she sang in the Auditorium. And there she goes on throwing it away on people who don't know what they are hearing."

"Rachel won't come here unless she can do it and keep her pledge at the same time," said Felicia after a pause.

"A very peculiar thing, that," Mr. Sterling said. "I wonder what Dr. Bruce thinks of it on the whole. I must have a talk with him."

"He is at home and will preach tomorrow," said Felicia. "Perhaps he will tell us something about it."

"Oh, well, let's have some tea!" said Rose, walking into the dining room. Her father and Felicia followed, and the meal proceeded in silence. Mrs. Sterling had her meals served in her room. Mr. Sterling was preoccupied. He ate very little and excused himself early.

"Don't you think Father looks very much disturbed lately?" asked Felicia a little while after he had gone out.

"Oh, I don't know! I hadn't noticed anything unusual," replied Rose. After a silence she said, "Are you going to the play tonight, Felicia? Mrs. Delano will be here at half past seven."

"I'll go. I don't care about it. I can see shadows enough without going to the play."

"That's a doleful remark for a girl nineteen years old to make," replied Rose. "If you are going up to see Mother, tell her I'll run in after the play if she is still awake."

Chapter 22

When the company was seated in the box and the curtain had gone up, Felicia was back of the others and remained for the evening by herself. Mrs. Delano, as chaperone for half a dozen young ladies, understood Felicia well enough to know that she was "peculiar," and she made no attempt to draw her out of her corner.

The play was an English melodrama full of startling situations, realistic scenery, and unexpected climaxes. One scene in the third act impressed even Rose Sterling.

It was midnight on Blackfriars Bridge. The Thames flowed dark and forbidding below. The figure of a child came upon the bridge and stood there for a moment peering about as if looking for someone. In one of the recesses about midway of the bridge a woman stood, leaning out over the parapet, with a strained agony of face and figure that told plainly of her intention. Just as she stealthily mounted the parapet to throw herself into the river, the child caught sight of her, ran forward with a shrill cry more animal than human, seized the woman's dress, and dragged back upon it with all her little strength.

Then there came suddenly upon the scene two other characters—a tall, handsome, athletic gentleman dressed in the fashion attended by a slim-figured lad who was as refined in dress and appearance as the little girl clinging to her mother, who was mournfully hideous in her rags and repulsive poverty. The gentleman and the lad prevented the attempted suicide, and after the revelation that the man and woman were brother and sister, the scene transferred to the interior of one of the slum tenements in the East Side of London.

Here the scene painter and carpenter had done their utmost to produce an exact copy of a famous court and alley well known to the poor creatures who make up a part of the outcast London humanity. The rags, the crowding, the vileness, the broken furniture, the horrible animal existence forced upon creatures made in God's image were so skillfully shown in this scene that more than one elegant woman in the theater caught herself shrinking back a little as if contamination were possible from the nearness of this piece of scenery.

From the tenement scene the play shifted to the interior of a nobleman's palace. The contrast was startling.

Felicia found herself living the scenes on the bridge and in the slums over and over. This was not the first time she had felt the contrast between the upper and the lower conditions of human life. It had been growing upon her until it had made her what Rose called "peculiar" and other people in her circle of wealthy acquaintances called "very unusual."

Finally, the play was over, the curtain down, and people went noisily out, laughing and gossiping as if *The Shadows of London* was simply good diversion.

Felicia rose and went out with the rest quietly. She was never absentminded but often thought herself into a condition that left her alone in the midst of a crowd.

"Well, what did you think of it?" asked Rose when the sisters had reached home and were in the drawing room.

"I thought it was a pretty fair picture of real life."

"I mean the acting," said Rose, annoyed.

"The bridge scene was well acted, especially the woman's part. I thought the man overdid the sentiment a little."

"Did you? I enjoyed that. But the slum scene was horrible. I think they ought not to show such things in a play. They are too painful."

"They must be painful in real life, too," replied Felicia.

"Yes, but we don't have to look at the real thing. It's bad enough at the theater where we pay for it."

"Are you going up to see Mother?" asked Felicia after a while.

"No," replied Rose. "I won't trouble her tonight. If you go in, tell her I am too tired to be agreeable."

So Felicia turned into her mother's room as she went up the great staircase and down the upper hall. The light burned there, and the servant who always waited on Mrs. Sterling beckoned Felicia to come in.

"Tell Clara to go out," Mrs. Sterling said as Felicia came up to the bed.

Surprised, Felicia did as her mother bade her and then inquired how she was feeling.

"Felicia," said her mother, "can you pray?"

The question was so unlike any her mother had ever asked before that she was startled. But she answered, "Why, yes, Mother. Why?"

"Felicia, I am frightened. Your father—I have had such strange fears about him all day. Something is wrong with him. I want you to pray."

"Now, here, Mother?"

"Yes. Pray, Felicia."

Felicia reached out her hand and took her mother's. It was trembling. Mrs. Sterling had never shown such tenderness for her younger daughter, and her strange demand now was the first real sign of any confidence in Felicia's character.

The girl knelt, still holding her mother's trembling hand, and prayed. She must have said in her prayer the words that her mother needed, for when it was silent in the room, the invalid wept softly and her nervous tension was over.

Felicia stayed some time. When she was assured that her mother would not need her any longer, she rose to go.

"Good night, Mother. You must let Clara call me if you feel badly in the night."

"I feel better now." Then as Felicia was moving away, Mrs. Sterling said, "Won't you kiss me, Felicia?"

Felicia went back and bent over her mother. The kiss was almost as strange to her as the prayer had been. When Felicia went out of the room, her cheeks were wet with tears.

Sunday morning at the Sterling mansion was generally very quiet. The girls went to eleven o'clock service at church. Mr. Sterling was not a member but a heavy contributor, and he generally went to church in the morning. Today he did not come down to breakfast and finally sent word by a servant that he did not feel well enough to go out. So Rose and Felicia drove up to the door of the Nazareth Avenue Church and entered the family pew alone.

Dr. Bruce walked out of the room at the rear of the platform and went up to the pulpit to open the Bible as his custom was. He proceeded with the service as usual. He was calm and his voice was steady and firm. His prayer was the first intimation the people had of anything new or strange in the service.

No one in Nazareth Avenue Church had any idea that Dr. Bruce, the dignified, cultured, refined doctor of divinity, had within a few days been crying like a little child on his knees, asking for strength and courage and Christlikeness to speak his Sunday message; and yet the prayer was an unconscious involuntary disclosure of his soul's experience such as the Nazareth Avenue people had seldom heard.

In the hush that succeeded the prayer, a distinct wave of spiritual power moved over the congregation. The most oblivious persons in the church felt it. Felicia, whose sensitive religious nature responded swiftly to every touch of emotion, quivered under the passing of that supernatural pressure, and when she lifted her head and looked up at the minister, there was a look in her eyes that announced her intense, eager anticipation of the scene that was to follow.

Chapter 23

"I am just back from a visit to Raymond," Dr. Bruce began, "and I want to tell you something of my impressions of the movement there."

He paused, and his look went out over his people with yearning for them but also uncertainty. Nevertheless, he had been through his desert and had come out of it ready to suffer. He went on now after that brief pause and told them the story of his stay in Raymond.

Dr. Bruce told his people simply and with a personal interest that led the way to the announcement that now followed. Felicia listened to every word with strained attention.

"Dear friends," he said, and for the first time since his prayer, the emotion of the occasion was revealed in his voice and gesture, "I am going to ask that Nazareth Avenue Church take the same pledge that Raymond Church has taken. I know what this will mean to you and me. It will mean what following Jesus meant in the first century, and then it meant suffering, loss, hardship, separation from everything unchristian. Those of us who volunteer in this church to do as Jesus would do simply promise to walk in His steps as He gave us commandment."

Again he paused, and now the result of his announcement was plainly visible in the stir that went up over the congregation. He added in a quiet voice that all who volunteered to make the pledge to do as Jesus would do were asked to remain after the morning service.

He then proceeded with his sermon. His text was "Master, I will follow Thee whithersoever Thou goest." The sermon was a revelation to the people of the definition their pastor had been learning. It was such a sermon as a man can preach once in a lifetime, and with enough in it for people to live on all through the rest of their lives.

The service closed in a hush that slowly broke. People rose here and there, a few at a time. Rose, however, walked straight out of the pew, and as she reached the aisle she turned her head and beckoned to Felicia.

"I am going to stay," she said, and Rose knew that her resolve could not be changed. Nevertheless, she went back into the pew two or three steps and faced her.

"Felicia," she whispered, and there was a flush of anger on her cheeks, "this is folly. You will bring some disgrace on the family. What will Father say? Come!"

Felicia looked at her but did not answer at once. She shook her head. "No, I am going to stay. I shall take the pledge. I am ready to obey it."

Rose gave her one look, then turned and went out of the pew and down the aisle.

❧

When Rose reached home, her father stood in his usual attitude before the open fireplace, smoking a cigar.

"Where is Felicia?" he asked as Rose came in.

"She stayed to an after-meeting," replied Rose shortly. She threw off her wraps and was going upstairs when Mr. Sterling called after her.

"An after-meeting? What do you mean?"

"Dr. Bruce asked the church to take the Raymond pledge."

Mr. Sterling took his cigar out of his mouth and twirled it nervously between his fingers.

"I didn't expect that of him. Did many of the members stay?"

"I don't know. I didn't," replied Rose, and she went upstairs, leaving her father standing in the drawing room.

After a few moments he went to the window and stood there looking out at the people driving on the boulevard. His cigar had gone out, but he still fingered it nervously. Then he turned from the window and walked up and down the room. A servant stepped across the hall and announced dinner, and he told her to wait for Felicia. Finally wearied of the walking, he threw himself into a chair and was brooding over something deeply when Felicia came in.

He rose and faced her. Felicia was evidently very much moved by the meeting from which she had just come. At the same time, she did not wish to talk too much about it. Just as she entered the drawing room, Rose came in.

"How many stayed?" Rose asked.

"About a hundred," replied Felicia gravely.

Mr. Sterling looked surprised. Felicia went out of the room, but he called to her. "Do you really mean to keep the pledge?" he asked.

Felicia colored. "You would not ask such a question, Father, if you had been at the meeting." She lingered a moment in the room, then asked to be excused from dinner for a while and went up to see her mother.

❁

That same evening, after the Sunday evening service, Dr. Bruce talked over the events of the day with his wife. They were of one heart and mind in the matter and faced their new future with all the faith and courage of new disciples.

The bell rang and Dr. Bruce, going to the door, exclaimed as he opened it, "It is you, Edward! Come in."

A commanding figure stepped into the hall. The Bishop was of extraordinary height and breadth of shoulder but of such good proportions that there was no thought of ungainly or even of unusual size.

He came into the parlor and greeted Mrs. Bruce, who after a few moments was called out of the room, leaving the two men together. The Bishop sat in a deep easy chair before the open fire. "Calvin, you have taken a very serious step today," he finally said, lifting his large dark eyes to his old college classmate's face. "I heard of it this afternoon. I could not resist the desire to see you about it tonight."

"I'm glad you came. You understand what this means, Edward?"

"Yes." The Bishop spoke very slowly and thoughtfully. He sat with his hands clasped together. Over his face, marked with lines of consecration and service and the love of men, a shadow crept. Again he lifted his eyes toward his old friend.

"Calvin, we have always understood each other. Ever since our paths led us in different ways in church life, we have walked together in Christian fellowship."

"It is true," replied Dr. Bruce with an emotion he made no attempt to conceal or subdue. "Thank God for it. I prize your fellowship more than any other man's."

The Bishop looked affectionately at his friend. But the shadow still rested on his face. After a pause he spoke again. "The new discipleship means a crisis for you in your work. If you keep this pledge to do all things as Jesus would do—as I know you will—it requires no prophet to predict some remarkable changes in your parish." The Bishop looked wistfully at his friend and then continued. "In fact, I do not see how a perfect upheaval of Christianity, as we now know it, can be prevented if the ministers and churches generally take the Raymond pledge and live it out." There flashed into Dr. Bruce's mind a suspicion of the truth. What if the Bishop would throw the weight of his great influence on the side of the Raymond movement? Dr. Bruce reached out his hand and, with the familiarity of lifelong friendship, placed it on the Bishop's shoulder. But before he could speak, they were both startled by the violent ringing of the bell.

Mrs. Bruce went to the door and talked with someone in the hall. There was a loud exclamation, and then, as the Bishop rose and Bruce stepped toward the curtain that hung before the entrance to the parlor, Mrs. Bruce pushed it aside. Her face was white and she was trembling.

"Oh, Calvin! Such terrible news! Mr. Sterling—oh, I cannot tell it! What a blow to those girls!"

"What is it?" Mr. Bruce advanced with the Bishop into the hall and confronted the messenger, a servant from the Sterlings. The man was without his hat and had evidently run over with the news.

"Mr. Sterling shot himself, sir, a few minutes ago. He killed himself in his bedroom. Mrs. Sterling—"

"I will go right over. Edward, will you go with me? The Sterlings are old friends of yours."

The Bishop was very pale but calm as always. "Aye, Calvin, I will go with you, not only to this house of death, but also the whole way of human sin and sorrow, please God."

Chapter 24

When Dr. Bruce and the Bishop entered the Sterling mansion, everything in the usually well-appointed household was in the greatest confusion and terror. The great rooms downstairs were empty, but overhead they heard hurried footsteps and confused noises. One of the servants ran down the grand staircase with a look of horror on her face just as the Bishop and Dr. Bruce started to go up.

"Miss Felicia is with Mrs. Sterling," the servant stammered in answer to a question, and then burst into a hysterical cry and ran through the drawing room and out of doors.

At the top of the staircase, Felicia met the two men. She walked up to Dr. Bruce at once and put both hands in his. The Bishop then laid his hand on her head, and the three stood there a moment in perfect silence. The Bishop had known Felicia since she was a little child. He was the first to break the silence.

"The God of all mercy be with you, Felicia, in this dark hour. Your mother—" The Bishop hesitated.

Answering the Bishop's unfinished query, Felicia turned and went back into her mother's room. But both men were struck with her wonderful calm as they followed her.

Rose lay with her arms outstretched upon the bed. Clara, the nurse, sat with her head covered, sobbing in spasms of terror. And Mrs. Sterling lay there so still that the Bishop was deceived at first. Then, as the great truth broke upon him, he staggered.

The next moment the house below was in a tumult. Almost at the same time, the doctor came in together with a police officer, both summoned by frightened servants. Four or five newspaper correspondents and several neighbors came in with them. Dr. Bruce and the Bishop met this miscellaneous crowd at the head of the stairs and succeeded in excluding all except those whose presence was necessary. With these the two friends learned all the facts ever known about the "Sterling tragedy," as the papers in their sensational accounts the next day called it.

Mr. Sterling had gone into his room that evening about nine o'clock, and that was the last seen of him until, a half hour later, a shot was heard in the room. A servant who was in the hall ran into the room and found him dead on the floor, killed by his own hand. Felicia at the time was sitting by her mother. Rose was reading in the library. She ran upstairs, saw her father as the servants lifted him to the couch, and then ran screaming into her mother's room, where she flung herself down at the foot of the bed in a swoon. Mrs. Sterling at first fainted at the shock, then rallied with a wonderful swiftness and sent for Dr. Bruce. She then insisted on seeing her husband. In spite of Felicia's efforts, she compelled Clara to support her while she crossed the hall and entered the room where her husband lay. She looked upon him with a tearless face, went back to her own room, was laid on her bed, and as Dr. Bruce and the Bishop entered the house, she died, with Felicia bending over her and Rose still lying senseless at her feet.

When the facts regarding Mr. Sterling's business affairs were disclosed, they learned that for some time he had been facing financial ruin owing to certain speculations that swept his supposed wealth into complete destruction. Sunday afternoon, he received news that proved to him beyond a doubt the fact of his utter ruin. The very house that he called his, the chairs in which he sat, his carriage, the dishes from which he ate, all rested on a tissue of deceit and speculation that had no foundation in real values. As soon as the truth that he was practically a beggar had dawned upon him, he saw no escape from suicide. Mrs. Sterling's death was the result of the shock. She had not been taken into her husband's confidence for years, but she knew that the source of his wealth was precarious. When she was carried into the room where her husband lay, her feeble tenement could not hold the spirit, and it gave up the ghost, torn and weakened by long years of suffering and disappointment.

The horror of events stupefied Rose for weeks. She lay unmoved by sympathy or any effort to rally. Even when she was told that she and Felicia must leave the house and be dependent on relatives and friends, she didn't seem to understand what it meant.

Felicia, however, was fully conscious of the facts. Mrs. Winslow and Rachel left Raymond and came to Chicago as soon as the terrible news had reached them, and they now planned for Rose and Felicia's future.

So in a few weeks Rose and Felicia found themselves a part of the Winslow family in Raymond. It was a bitter experience for Rose, but there was nothing else for her to do, and she accepted the inevitable, brooding over the great change in her life and in many ways adding to Felicia's and Rachel's burden.

Felicia at once found herself in an atmosphere of discipleship that was like heaven to her in its revelation of companionship. In the spirit of her new life, she insisted upon helping in the housework at her aunt's, and in a short time demonstrated her ability as a cook so clearly that Virginia suggested that she take charge of the cooking at the Rectangle.

Felicia entered upon this work with the keenest pleasure. For the first time in her life, she had the delight of doing something of value for the happiness of others. Her resolve to do everything after asking, "What would Jesus do?" touched her deepest nature. She developed and strengthened wonderfully.

Even Mrs. Winslow was obliged to acknowledge the great usefulness and beauty of Felicia's character. The aunt looked with astonishment upon her niece, this city-bred girl, reared in the greatest luxury, the daughter of a millionaire, now walking around in her kitchen, her arms covered with flour and occasionally a streak of it on her nose, for Felicia at first had a habit of rubbing her nose forgetfully when she was trying to remember some recipe, mixing various dishes with the greatest interest in their results, washing up pans and kettles, and doing the ordinary work of a servant in the Winslow kitchen and at the rooms at the Rectangle Settlement.

Felicia grew into the affections of Raymond people and the Rectangle folks, among whom she was known as the "angel cook." Underneath the structure of the beautiful character she was growing, always rested her promise made in Nazareth Avenue Church. "What would Jesus do?"

Chapter 25

Three months of great excitement followed the Sunday morning when Dr. Bruce came into his pulpit with the message of the new discipleship. Rev. Calvin Bruce hadn't realized how deep the feeling of his members flowed. He humbly confessed that the appeal he had made met with an unexpected response from men and women who were hungry for something in their lives that the conventional type of church membership and fellowship had failed to give them.

But Dr. Bruce was not yet satisfied for himself. One evening the Bishop joined Dr. Bruce in his study.

They talked for some time about the results of the pledge with the Nazareth Avenue people before the Bishop asked his friend, "You know why I've come to you this evening?"

Dr. Bruce shook his head.

"I have come to confess that I have not yet kept my promise to walk in His steps in the way that I believe I shall be obliged to if I satisfy my thought of what it means to walk in His steps."

Dr. Bruce rose and paced his study. The Bishop remained in the deep easy chair with his hands clasped, eyes glowing with determination.

"Edward"—Dr. Bruce spoke abruptly—"I have not yet been able to satisfy myself, either, in obeying my promise. But I have at last decided on my course. In order to follow it, I shall be obliged to resign from Nazareth Avenue Church."

"I knew you would," replied the Bishop quietly. "And I came in this evening to say that I shall be obliged to do the same thing with my charge."

Dr. Bruce turned and walked up to his friend. "Is it necessary in your case?" asked Bruce.

"Yes. Let me state my reasons. I'm sure they are the same as yours." The Bishop paused a moment, then went on with increasing feeling. "Calvin, you know how many years I have been doing the work of my position, and you know something of the responsibility and care of it. I do not mean to say that my life has been free from burden bearing or sorrow. But I have certainly led what the poor and desperate of this sinful city would call a very comfortable, yes, a very luxurious life. And I have been unable to silence the question of late: 'What have I suffered for the sake of Christ?' Maxwell's position at Raymond is well taken when he insists that to walk in the steps of Christ means to suffer. Compared with Paul or any of the Christian martyrs or early disciples, I have lived a luxurious, sinful life, full of ease and pleasure. I cannot endure this any longer. I have not been walking in His steps. Under the present system of church and social life, I see no escape from this condemnation except to give the most of my life personally to the actual physical and soul needs of the wretched people in the worst part of this city."

The Bishop rose and walked over to the window. The street in front of the house was as light as day, and he looked out at the crowds passing, then turned, and with a passionate utterance that showed how deep the volcanic fire in him burned, he exclaimed, "Calvin, this is a terrible city in which we live! Its misery, its sin, its selfishness appall my heart. The awful conditions of the girls in some great business places, the fearful curse of the drink and gambling hall, the wail of the unemployed, the countless men who see in the church only great piles of costly stone and upholstered furniture and the minister as a luxurious idler—all this as a total fact in its contrast with the easy, comfortable life I have lived fills me more and more with a sense of mingled terror and self-accusation. What have I suffered for Jesus' sake?" Dr. Bruce was very pale. Never had he seen the Bishop or heard him when under the influence of such a passion. There was a sudden silence in the room. The Bishop sat down again and bowed his head.

Dr. Bruce spoke at last: "Edward, I do not need to say that you have expressed my feelings also. I have been in a similar position for years. I cannot say that I have suffered any for Jesus. That verse in Peter constantly haunts me: 'Christ also suffered for us, leaving us an example, that ye should follow his steps.' The sin and misery of this great city have beaten like waves against the stone wall of my church and of this house in which I live, and I have hardly heeded them, the walls have been so thick. I have reached a point where I cannot endure this any longer. I am not condemning the Church. I love her. I am not forsaking the Church. I believe in her mission and have no desire to destroy. Least of all in the step I am about to take do I desire to be charged with abandoning the Christian fellowship. But I feel that I must resign my place as pastor of Nazareth Church in order to satisfy myself that I am walking as I ought to walk in His steps. I must come personally into a close contact with the sin and shame and degradation of this great city. And I know that to do that I must sever my immediate connection with Nazareth Avenue Church."

Again that sudden silence fell over those two men. It was no ordinary action they were deciding. "What is your plan?" The Bishop at last spoke gently, looking with the smile that always beautified his face.

"My plan," replied Dr. Bruce slowly, "is to put myself into the center of the greatest human need I can find in this city and live there. My wife is fully in accord with me. We have already decided to find a residence in that part of the city where we can make our personal lives count for the most."

"Let me suggest a place." He went on and unfolded a plan of such far-reaching power and possibility that Dr. Bruce, capable and experienced as he was, felt amazed at the vision of a greater soul than his own.

They sat up late working out the details. Their plan as it finally grew into a workable fact was in reality nothing more than renting a large building formerly used as a warehouse for a brewery, reconstructing it, and living in it in the very heart of a territory where the saloon ruled with power, where the tenement was its filthiest, where vice and ignorance and shame and poverty were congested into hideous forms. The two friends agreed to pool their money to finance the work, most of it going into the furnishing of the Settlement House.

Chapter 26

At Nazareth Avenue Church the simple appeal on the part of its pastor to his members to do as Jesus would do had created a sensation that still continued. Then Dr. Bruce came into his pulpit and announced his resignation, and the sensation deepened all over the city. When it became publicly known that the Bishop had also announced his resignation and retirement from the position he had held so long in order to go and live himself in the center of the worst part of Chicago, the public astonishment reached its height.

"Why should what Dr. Bruce and I propose to do seem so remarkable a thing?" the Bishop asked one valued friend who had almost with tears tried to dissuade him from his purpose. "If we were to resign our charge for the purpose of going to Bombay or Hong Kong or any place in Africa, the churches and the people would exclaim at the heroism of missions. Why should it seem so great a thing if we have been led to give our lives to help rescue the heathen and the lost of our own city in the way we are going to try it?"

But the public continued to talk, and the churches recorded their astonishment that two such men, so prominent in the ministry, should leave their comfortable homes, voluntarily resign their pleasant social positions, and enter upon a life of hardship, self-denial, and actual suffering.

❀

It was fall again when the Bishop came out of the Settlement one afternoon and walked around the block, intending to go on a visit to one of his new friends in the district. He had walked about four blocks when he noticed a shop that looked different from the others—a small house close by a Chinese laundry. There were two windows in the front, very clean. Then, inside the window, was a tempting display of cookery, with prices attached to the various articles that made him wonder somewhat, for he was familiar by this time with many facts in the life of the people once unknown to him. As he stood looking at the windows, the door between them opened and Felicia Sterling came out.

"Felicia!" exclaimed the Bishop.

"How did you find me so soon?" inquired Felicia.

"Why, don't you know? These are the only clean windows in the block."

"I believe they are," replied Felicia with a laugh that did the Bishop good to hear.

"But why have you dared to come to Chicago without telling me, and how have you entered my diocese without my knowledge?" asked the Bishop.

"Well, dear Bishop," said Felicia, who had always called him so, "I was just on my way to see you and ask your advice. I am settled here for the present with Mrs. Bascom, a saleswoman who rents out three rooms, and with one of Rachel's music pupils to whom Virginia Page has given a course of study in violin. She is from the people," continued Felicia, "and I am keeping house for her and at the same time beginning an experiment in pure food for the masses. I am an expert, and I have a plan I want you to admire and develop. Will you, dear Bishop?"

"Indeed I will," he replied.

"Martha can help at the Settlement with her violin, and I will help with my messes. You see, I thought I would get settled first and work out something, and then come with some real thing to offer. I'm able to earn my own living now."

"You are?" the Bishop said a little incredulously. "How? Making those things?"

"Those things!" said Felicia with a show of indignation. "I would have you know, sir, that 'those things' are the best-cooked, purest food products in this whole city."

"I don't doubt it," he replied hastily, while his eyes twinkled. "Still, 'the proof of the pudding'—you know the rest."

"Come in and try some!" she exclaimed. "You poor Bishop! You look as if you haven't had a good meal for a month."

So they had an improvised lunch, and the Bishop, who, to tell the truth, had not taken time for weeks to enjoy his meals, feasted on the delight of his unexpected discovery and was able to express his astonishment and gratification at the quality of the cookery.

"Felicia, you must come to the Settlement. I want you to see what we are doing. And I am simply astonished to find you here earning your living this way. You don't really mean that you will live here and help these people to know the value of good food?"

"Indeed I do," she answered gravely. "That is my gospel. Shall I not follow it?"

"Aye, aye! You're right. Bless God for sense like yours!"

Felicia went back with him to visit the Settlement. She was amazed at the results of what considerable money and a good deal of consecrated brains had done. As they walked through the building, they talked incessantly. She was the incarnation of vital enthusiasm, and he wondered at the exhibition of it as it bubbled up and sparkled over.

They went down into the basement, and the Bishop pushed open a door. It was a small but well-equipped carpenter's shop. A young man with a paper cap on his head and clad in blouse and overalls was driving a plane as he whistled. He looked up as the two entered, and took off his cap. As he did so, his little finger carried a small curled shaving up to his hair and it caught there.

"Miss Sterling, Mr. Stephen Clyde," said the Bishop. "Clyde is one of our helpers here two afternoons in the week."

Just then the Bishop was called upstairs, and he excused himself a moment, leaving Felicia and the young carpenter together.

"We have met before," said Felicia, looking at Clyde frankly.

"Yes, 'back in the world,' as the Bishop says," replied the young man, and his fingers trembled a little as they lay on the board he had been planing.

"Yes." Felicia hesitated. "I am very glad to see you."

"Are you?" The flush of pleasure mounted to the young carpenter's forehead. "You have had a great deal of trouble since—since—then," he said.

"Yes, and you also. How is it that you're working here?"

"My father lost his money, and I was obliged to go to work. A very good thing for me. I learned the trade, hoping sometime to be of use. I am night clerk at one of the hotels. That Sunday morning when you took the pledge at Nazareth Avenue Church, I took it with the others."

"Did you?" said Felicia slowly. "I am glad."

Just then the Bishop came back, and very soon he and Felicia went away, leaving the young carpenter at his work.

"Felicia," said the Bishop, "did you know Stephen Clyde before?"

"Yes, 'back in the world,' dear Bishop. He was one of my acquaintances in Nazareth Avenue Church."

"Ah!" said the Bishop.

"We were very good friends," added Felicia.

"But nothing more?" the Bishop ventured to ask.

Felicia's face glowed for an instant. Then she looked her companion in the eyes frankly and answered, "Truly, nothing more."

Chapter 27

The following week, the Bishop was coming back to the Settlement very late when two men jumped out from behind an old fence that shut off an abandoned factory from the street. One of the men thrust a pistol in his face, and the other threatened him with a ragged stake that had been torn from the fence.

"Hold up your hands, and be quick about it!" said the man with the pistol.

He did as he was commanded, and the man with the stake began to go through his pockets.

The Bishop was not in the habit of carrying much money with him, and the man searching him uttered an oath at the small amount of change he found. As he uttered it, the man with the pistol savagely said, "Jerk out his watch! We might as well get all we can out of the job!"

"The chain is caught somewhere!" and the other man swore again.

"Break it, then!"

"No, don't break it," the Bishop said. "The chain is the gift of a very dear friend."

At the sound of the Bishop's voice, the man with the pistol started. With a quick movement of his other hand, he turned the Bishop's head toward what little light was shining from the alleyway, at the same time taking a step nearer. Then he said roughly, "Leave the watch alone! We've got the money. That's enough!"

"Enough! Fifty cents! You don't reckon—"

Before the man with the stake could say another word, he was confronted with the muzzle of the pistol turned from the Bishop's head toward his own.

"Leave that watch be! And put back the money, too. This is the Bishop we've held up."

"And what of it! The president of the United States wouldn't be too good to hold up, if—"

"I say, you put the money back, or in five seconds I'll blow a hole through your head that'll let in more sense than you have to spare now!" said the other.

For a second the man with the stake seemed to hesitate; then he hastily dropped the money back into the rifled pocket.

"You can take your hands down, sir." The man lowered his weapon slowly, still keeping an eye on the other man.

The Bishop slowly brought his arms to his sides and looked earnestly at the two men. In the dim light it was difficult to distinguish features.

"You can go on. You needn't stay any longer on our account." The man who had acted as spokesman turned and sat down on a stone. The other man stood viciously digging his stake into the ground.

"That's just what I am staying for," replied the Bishop. He sat down on a board that projected from the broken fence.

"You must like our company."

"If you would only allow me to be of any help." The Bishop spoke gently.

The man on the stone stared at the Bishop through the darkness. After a moment of silence, he spoke slowly.

"Do you remember ever seeing me before?"

"No," said the Bishop. "The light is not very good, and I have really not had a good look at you."

"Do you know me now?" The man suddenly took off his hat and, getting up from the stone, walked over to the Bishop until they were near enough to touch each other.

The man's hair was coal black except one spot on the top of his head as large as the palm of the hand, which was white.

The minute the Bishop saw that, he started. A memory of fifteen years ago stirred in him.

"Don't you remember one day back in '81 or '82 a man came to your house and told a story about his wife and child having been burned to death in a tenement fire in New York?"

"Yes."

"Do you remember how you took me into your own house that night and spent all the next day trying to find me a job? And how when you succeeded in getting me a place in a warehouse as foreman, I promised to quit drinking because you asked me to?"

"I remember it now. I hope you have kept your promise."

The man laughed savagely. "Kept it! I was drunk inside of a week! But I've never forgotten you or your prayer. Do you remember the morning after I came to your house, after breakfast you had prayers and asked me to come in and sit with the rest? My mother used to pray! I can see her now kneeling down by my bed when I was a lad. I never forgot that prayer of yours that morning. You prayed for me just as Mother used to, and you didn't seem to take 'count of the fact that I was ragged and tough-looking and more than half drunk when I rang your doorbell. My promise not to drink was broken into a thousand pieces inside of two Sundays, and I lost the job you found for me and landed in a police station two days later." The man put his hat back on and sat down on the stone again.

The Bishop did not stir. Somewhere a church clock struck one. "How long is it since you had work?" he asked.

The man standing up answered. "More'n six months since either of us did anything to tell of, unless you count 'holding up' work. I call it a pretty wearing kind of a job myself, especially when we put in a night like this and don't make nothin'."

"Suppose I found good jobs for both of you? Would you quit this and begin all over?"

"What's the use?" The man on the stone spoke sullenly. "I've reformed a hundred times. Every time I go down deeper. It's too late."

"No!" said the Bishop. And never before had he felt the desire for souls burn up in him so strongly. "No!" the Bishop repeated.

"What does God want of you two men? He wants just what I do in this case. You two are of infinite value to Him." And then his wonderful memory came to his aid. He remembered the man's name in spite of the busy years that lay between his coming to the house and the present moment.

"Burns," he said, "if you and your friend here will go home with me tonight, I will find you both places of honorable employment. I will believe in you and trust you. Why should God lose you? But if you need to feel again that there is love in the world, you will believe me when I say, my brothers, that I love you, and in the name of Him who was crucified for our sins, I cannot bear to see you miss the glory of the human life. Come, be men! Make another try for it, God helping you. No one but God and you and myself need ever know anything of this tonight. It was the sinner that Christ came to help. I'll do what I can for you. O God, give me the souls of these two men!"

And he broke into a prayer to God that was a continuation of his appeal to the men. His pent-up feeling had no other outlet. The prayer seemed to break open the crust that for years had surrounded them and shut them off from divine communication. And they themselves were thoroughly startled by it.

The Bishop ceased. Burns still sat with his head bowed between his knees. The man leaning against the fence looked at the Bishop with a face in which new emotions of awe, repentance, astonishment, and joy struggled for expression. The Bishop rose.

"Come, my brothers. God is good. You shall stay at the Settlement tonight, and I will make good my promise as to the work."

The two men followed him in silence. When they reached the Settlement, it was after two o'clock. He let them in and led them to a room.

"God bless you, my brothers!" he said, and leaving them his benediction, he went away.

True to his promise he secured work for them. The janitor at the Settlement needed an assistant, owing to the growth of the work there. So Burns was given the place. The Bishop succeeded in getting his companion a position as driver for a firm of warehouse dray manufacturers not far from the Settlement. And the Holy Spirit began His marvelous work of regeneration.

Chapter 28

Later that afternoon Burns was cleaning off the front steps of the Settlement when he paused a moment and stood up to look about him. The first thing he noticed was a beer sign just across the alley. Immediately opposite were two large saloons.

Suddenly the door of the nearest saloon opened, and a strong odor of beer floated up to Burns as he stood on the steps. He took another step down, still sweeping. The sweat stood on his forehead although the day was frosty. Then he pulled himself up one step and swept over the spot he had just cleaned. Then, by a tremendous effort, dragged himself back to the floor of the porch and went over into the corner of it farthest from the saloon and began to sweep there. He swept in the corner for two or three minutes, his face drawn with the agony of his conflict. Gradually he edged out again toward the steps and began to go down them. He looked toward the sidewalk and saw he had left one step unswept. The sight seemed to give him a reasonable excuse for going down there to finish his sweeping.

He was on the sidewalk now, sweeping the last step, with his face toward the Settlement and his back turned partly on the saloon across the alley. He swept the step a dozen times. The sweat rolled over his face and dropped down at his feet.

He was down in the middle of the sidewalk now, still sweeping. He cleared the space in front of the Settlement and even went out into the gutter and swept that. He took off his hat and rubbed his sleeve over his face. He trembled all over like a palsied man and staggered back and forth as if he were already drunk. His soul shook within him.

He crossed over the little piece of stone flagging that measured the width of the alley, and now he stood in front of the saloon, looking at the sign and staring into the window at the pile of whiskey and beer bottles arranged in a great pyramid inside. He moistened his lips with his tongue and took a step forward, looking around him stealthily. As he laid his fingers on the door handle, a tall figure came around the corner.

The Bishop seized Burns by the arm and dragged him back upon the sidewalk. The frenzied man, now mad for a drink, shrieked out a curse and struck at his friend savagely. The Bishop picked Burns up as if he had been a child and actually carried him up the steps and into the house. He put him down in the hall and then shut the door and put his back against it.

Burns fell on his knees sobbing and praying. The Bishop stood there panting with his exertion, moved with unspeakable pity.

"Pray, Burns—pray as you never prayed before! Nothing else will save you!"

"O God! Pray with me. Save me! Oh, save me from my hell!" cried Burns. And the Bishop knelt by him in the hall and prayed as only he could pray.

After that they rose, and Burns went to his room.

The Bishop went out on the porch. The air of the whole city seemed to be impregnated with the odor of beer. "How long, O Lord, how long?" he prayed.

When Dr. Bruce joined him, the Bishop asked, "Did you ever make any inquiries about the ownership of the property adjoining us?"

"No, I haven't taken time for it. I will now if you think it would be worthwhile. But what can we do, Edward, against the saloon in this great city? It is as firmly established as the churches or politics. What power can ever remove it?"

"God will do it in time, as He has removed slavery," was the grave reply. "Meanwhile I think we have a right to know who controls this saloon so near the Settlement."

"I'll find out," said Dr. Bruce.

❧

Two days later Dr. Bruce walked into the business office of one of the members of Nazareth Avenue Church and asked to see him a few moments. His old parishioner cordially welcomed him into his office.

"I called to see you about that property next to the Settlement where the Bishop and myself now are. I am going to speak plainly, because life is too short and too serious for us both to have any foolish hesitation about this matter. Clayton, do you think it is right to rent that property for a saloon?"

The effect of the question on his old parishioner was instantaneous.

The hot blood mounted to the face of the man. Then he grew pale and dropped his head on his hands, and when he raised it again, Dr. Bruce was amazed to see a tear roll over his face.

"Doctor, since I took the pledge that morning with the others, that saloon property has been the temptation of the devil to me. It is the best-paying investment at present that I have. And yet it was only a minute before you came in here that I was in an agony of remorse to think how I was letting a little earthly gain tempt me into a denial of the very Christ I had promised to follow. There is no need, Dr. Bruce, for you to say a word more."

Clayton held out his hand, and Dr. Bruce grasped it and shook it hard. Within a month the saloon next to the Settlement was closed. The saloonkeeper's lease expired, and Clayton not only closed the property to the whiskey men, but offered the building to the Bishop and Dr. Bruce to use for the Settlement work, which had now grown so large that the building they had first rented was not sufficient for the different industries that were planned.

Soon, Felicia found herself installed in the very room where souls had been lost, as head of the department not only of cooking but of a course of housekeeping for girls who wished to go out to service.

"Felicia, tell us your plan in full now," said the Bishop one evening when, in a rare interval of rest from the great pressure of work, he was with Dr. Bruce, and Felicia had come in from the other building.

"Well, I have long thought of the hired girl problem," said Felicia with an air of wisdom that made Mrs. Bruce smile. "So this is what I propose to do. The old saloon building is large enough to arrange into a suite of rooms that will represent an ordinary house. Once it is arranged, then I'll teach housekeeping and cooking to girls who will afterward go out to service. The course will be six months long. In that time I will teach plain cooking, neatness, quickness, and a love of good work."

"Hold on, Felicia!" the Bishop interrupted. "This is not an age of miracles!"

"Then we will make it one," replied Felicia. "I know this seems like an impossibility, but I want to try it. I know a score of girls already who will take the course, and if we can once establish something like an *esprit de corps* among the girls themselves, I am sure it will be of great value to them."

"Felicia, if you can accomplish half what you propose, it will bless this community," said Mrs. Bruce. "God bless you as you try."

With this blessing, Felicia plunged into the working out of her plan with the enthusiasm of her discipleship, which every day grew more and more practical and serviceable.

Chapter 29

The breakfast hour at the Settlement was the one hour in the day when the whole family found a little breathing space to fellowship together. It was an hour of relaxation. This particular morning the Bishop read extracts from a morning paper for the benefit of the others. Suddenly he paused, and his face instantly grew stern and sad. The rest looked up and a hush fell over the table.

"Shot and killed while taking a lump of coal from a car! His family was freezing and he had no work for six months. Six children and a wife all packed into a cabin with three rooms, on the West Side. One child wrapped in rags in a closet!"

These were headlines that he read slowly. He then went on and read the detailed account of the shooting and the visit of the reporter to the tenement where the family lived. He finished, and there was silence around the table. "How awful! Where is the place, did you say?" asked Mrs. Bruce.

"It is only three blocks from here. I believe Penrose owns half of the houses in that block. They are among the worst houses in this part of the city. And Penrose is a church member."

"Yes, he belongs to the Nazareth Avenue Church," replied Dr. Bruce in a low voice.

Just as the Bishop rose from the table, the very figure of divine wrath, the bell rang and one of the residents went to the door.

"Tell Dr. Bruce and the Bishop I want to see them. Penrose is the name—Clarence Penrose."

The family at the breakfast table heard every word. The two men instantly left the table and went out into the hall.

"Come in here, Penrose," said Dr. Bruce, and they ushered the visitor into the reception room, closed the door, and were alone.

Clarence Penrose came from an aristocratic family of great wealth and social distinction. He was exceedingly wealthy and had large property holdings in different parts of the city. Now he faced the two ministers with a look of agitation on his face that showed plainly the mark of some unusual experience. He was very pale and his lips trembled. Penrose turned toward Dr. Bruce. "I came to say that I have had an experience so unusual that nothing but the supernatural can explain it. I was one of those who took the pledge to do as Jesus would do. And I have been living in a perfect hell of contradictions ever since. My little girl, Diana, also took the pledge with me. She's asking me a great many questions lately about the poor people and where they live. One of her questions last night touched my sore! 'Do you own any houses where these poor people live? Are they nice and warm like ours?' I went to bed, but I could not sleep. I seemed to see the judgment day. I was placed before the Judge and asked to give an account of my deeds done in the body. 'What had I done with my stewardship? How about those tenements where people froze in winter and stifled in summer? Did I give any thought to them except to receive the rentals from them? Where did my suffering come in? Would Jesus have done as I had done and was doing? Had I broken my pledge? How had I used the money and the culture and the social influence I possessed? Had I used it to bless humanity, to relieve the suffering, to bring joy to the distressed and hope to the despondent? I had received much. How much had I given?'

"All this came to me in a waking vision as distinctly as I see you two men and myself now. I had a confused picture in my mind of the suffering Christ pointing a condemning finger at me, and the rest was shut out by mist and darkness. Then the first thing I saw this morning was the account of the shooting at the coal yards. I read the account with a feeling of horror I have not been able to shake off. I am a guilty creature before God."

Penrose paused. The two men looked at him solemnly. Into that room came a breath such as before swept over Henry Maxwell's church and through Nazareth Avenue. The Bishop laid his hand on the shoulder of Penrose and said, "My brother, God has been very near to you. Let us thank Him."

"Yes! Yes!" sobbed Penrose. He sat down on a chair and covered his face. The Bishop prayed. Then Penrose quietly said, "Will you go with me to that house?"

For answer the two men put on their overcoats and went with him to the home of the dead man's family. From the moment he stepped into that wretched hovel of a home and faced for the first time in his life a despair and suffering such as he had read of but did not know by personal contact, he dated a new life.

❖

One afternoon just as Felicia came out of the Settlement with a basket of food that she was going to leave as a sample with a baker in the Penrose district, Stephen Clyde opened the door of the carpenter shop in the basement and came out in time to meet her as she reached the sidewalk.

"Let me carry your basket, please," he said.

"Why do you say 'please'?" asked Felicia, handing over the basket while they walked along.

"I would like to say something else," replied Stephen, glancing at her shyly and yet with a boldness that frightened him. He loved Felicia more every day since she stepped into the shop that day with the Bishop.

"What else?" asked Felicia, innocently falling into the trap.

"Why—," said Stephen, turning his fair, noble face full toward her. "I would like to say, 'Let me carry your basket, dear Felicia.'"

Felicia never looked so beautiful in her life. She walked on a little way without even turning her face toward him. It was no secret with her own heart that she had given it to Stephen some time ago. Finally, she turned and said shyly, while her face grew rosy and her eyes tender, "Why don't you say it, then?"

"May I?" cried Stephen, and he was so careless for a minute of the way he held the basket that Felicia exclaimed, "Yes! But oh, don't drop my goodies!"

"Why, I wouldn't drop anything so precious for all the world, dear Felicia," said Stephen, who now walked on air for several blocks.

Late in the afternoon, the Bishop, walking along quietly from the Penrose district, in rather a secluded spot near the outlying part of the Settlement district, heard a familiar voice say, "But tell me, Felicia, when did you begin to love me?"

"I fell in love with a little pine shaving just above your ear that day when I saw you in the shop!" said the other voice with a laugh so clear, so pure, so sweet that it did one good to hear it.

"Where are you going with that basket?" the Bishop tried to say sternly.

"We are taking it to—where are we taking it, Felicia?"

"Dear Bishop, we are taking it home to begin—"

"To begin housekeeping with," finished Stephen.

"Are you?" said the Bishop. "I hope you will invite me to share. I know what Felicia's cooking is."

"Bishop, dear Bishop!" said Felicia, and she did not pretend to hide her happiness. "Indeed, you shall be the most honored guest. Are you glad?"

"Yes, I am," he replied, interpreting Felicia's words as she wished. Then he paused a moment and said gently, "God bless you both!" and went his way with a tear in his eye and a prayer in his heart, and left them to their joy.

Chapter 30

Soon after this, the Bishop and Dr. Bruce invited Henry Maxwell of Raymond to come to Chicago to speak to a remarkable gathering at the hall of the Settlement. He brought several people from the First Church with him. It is doubtful if Mr. Maxwell ever faced such an audience in his life. It is quite certain that the city of Raymond did not contain such a variety of humanity.

The audience was respectfully attentive as he told in the simplest language he could command some of the results of obedience to the pledge as it had been taken in Raymond. As Mr. Maxwell went on, faces all over the hall leaned forward in a way seldom seen in church audiences or anywhere except among workingmen or the people of the street when once they are thoroughly aroused.

The Bishop and Dr. Bruce, looking on, saw many faces that represented scorn of creeds, hatred of the social order, desperate narrowness, and selfishness. They marveled that so soon under the influence of the Settlement life, the softening process already lightened the hearts of many who had grown bitter from neglect and indifference.

It was the custom at the Settlement for a free discussion to follow any open meeting of this kind. So when Mr. Maxwell finished and sat down, the Bishop rose and made the announcement that any man in the hall was at liberty to ask questions, to speak out his feelings, or to declare his convictions, always with the understanding that whoever took part was to observe the simple rules that governed parliamentary bodies and obey the three-minute rule, which would be enforced on account of the numbers present.

As soon as the Bishop sat down, two men began to talk at once.

The Bishop called them to order and indicated which was entitled to the floor. The man who remained standing began eagerly.

"This is the first time I was ever in here, and maybe it'll be the last. Fact is, I am about at the end of my string. I've tramped this city for work till I'm sick. I'd like to ask a question of the minister if it's fair. May I?"

"By all means," replied Mr. Maxwell quickly.

"This is my question." The man leaned forward and stretched out a long arm. "I want to know what Jesus would do in my case. I haven't had a stroke of work for two months. I've got a wife and three children, and I love them as much as if I was worth a million dollars. I've been living off a little earnings I saved up during the World's Fair jobs I got. I'm a carpenter by trade, and I've tried every way I know to get a job. I want to work. I've got to live, and my wife and my children have got to live. But how? What would Jesus do?"

Mr. Maxwell sat there staring at the great sea of faces all intent on his, and no answer to this man's question seemed possible. "O God!" his heart prayed. "What would Jesus do?"

At length Mr. Maxwell spoke. "Is there any man in the room, who is a Christian disciple, who has been in this condition and has tried to do as Jesus would do? If so, such a man can answer this question better than I can."

There was a moment's hush over the room, and then a man near the front of the hall slowly rose. He was an old man, and the hand he laid on the back of the bench in front of him shook as he spoke.

"I think I can safely say that I have many times been in just such a condition. I don't know as I have always asked this question, 'What would Jesus do?' when I have been out of work, but I do know I have tried to be His disciple at all times. Yes," the man went on, with a sad smile that was more pathetic than the younger man's grim despair, "yes, I have begged, and I have been to charity institutions, and I have done everything when out of a job except steal and lie in order to get food and fuel. I don't know as Jesus would have done some of the things I have been obliged to do for a living, but I know I have never knowingly done wrong when out of work."

A silence followed, broken by a fierce voice from a large, black-haired, heavily bearded man who sat three seats from the Bishop. The minute he spoke nearly every man in the hall leaned forward eagerly, anxious to hear what Carlsen, the Socialist leader, had to say.

"This is all bosh, to my mind," began Carlsen. His great bristling beard shook with the deep inward anger of the man. "The whole of our system is at fault. What we call civilization is rotten to the core. We live in an age of trusts and combines and capitalistic greed that means death to thousands of innocent men, women, and children. Yet this city, and every other big city in this country, has its thousands of professed Christians who have all the luxuries and comforts, and who go to church Sundays and sing their hymns about giving all to Jesus and bearing the cross and following Him all the way and being saved! I don't say that there aren't good men and women among them, but let the minister who has spoken to us here tonight go into any one of a dozen aristocratic churches I could name and propose to the members to take any such pledge as the one he's mentioned here tonight, and see how quick the people would laugh at him for a fool or a crank or a fanatic. I don't look for any reform worth anything to come out of the churches. What we need is a system that starts from the common basis of socialism, founded on the rights of the common people—"

Carlsen was launching himself into a regular oration, when the man just behind him pulled him down unceremoniously. Carlsen subsided with several mutterings in his beard, while the next several speakers gave their opinions as to the cause of and solutions to the social ills in the city.

Finally, the Bishop called time on the free-for-all and asked Rachel to sing.

When Rachel Winslow began to sing tonight at this Settlement meeting, she never prayed more deeply for results to come from her voice.

She chose the words, "Hark! The voice of Jesus calling, follow

Me, follow Me!"

Henry Maxwell remembered his first night at the Rectangle in the tent when Rachel sang the people quiet. The effect was the same here. Surely this audience had never heard such a melody. How could it? The men who had drifted in from the street sat entranced by a voice that "back in the world" never could be heard by the common people because the owner of it would charge two or three dollars for the privilege. The song poured out through the hall as free and glad as if it were a foretaste of salvation itself.

Chapter 31

Friday morning Henry Maxwell received an invitation from the pastor of one of the largest churches in Chicago to fill the pulpit for both morning and evening service.

He hesitated but finally accepted, seeing in it the hand of the Spirit's guiding power. He would prove the truth or falsity of the charge made against the church at the Settlement meeting.

Sunday morning the great church was filled to its utmost. Henry Maxwell, coming into the pulpit from an all-night vigil in prayer, felt the pressure of a great curiosity on the part of the people. With this curiosity was something deeper, more serious. In the knowledge that the Spirit's presence was his living strength, Mr. Maxwell brought his message to that church that day.

This morning the people felt the complete sincerity and humility of a man who had gone deep into the heart of a great truth.

After telling briefly of some results in his own church in Raymond since the pledge was taken, he went on to ask the question he had been asking since the Settlement meeting. He took for his theme the story out of Luke 18 of the young man who came to Jesus asking what he must do to obtain eternal life. Jesus had tested him. "Sell all that thou hast, and distribute unto the poor, and thou shalt have treasure in heaven: and come, follow me." But the young man was not willing to suffer to that extent. "Is it true," continued Henry Maxwell, and his fine, thoughtful face glowed with a passion of appeal that stirred the people as they had seldom been stirred, "that the church of today, the church that is called after Christ's own name, would refuse to follow Him at the expense of suffering, of physical loss, of temporary gain? The statement was made at a large gathering in the Settlement last week by a leader of workingmen that it was hopeless to look to the Church for any reform or redemption of society. Are the Christians of America ready to have their discipleship tested? How about the men who possess large wealth? Are they ready to take that wealth and use it as Jesus would? How about the men and women of great talent? Are they ready to consecrate that talent to humanity as Jesus undoubtedly would do?

"Would it not be true that if every Christian in America did as Jesus would do, society itself, the business world, yes, the very political system under which our commercial and government activity is carried on, would be so changed that human suffering would be reduced to a minimum?

"What is the test of Christian discipleship? If Jesus were here today, would He not call some of the members of this very church to do just what He commanded the young man, and ask them to give up their wealth and literally follow Him?

"What would be the result if in this city every church member should begin to do as Jesus would do? It is not easy to go into details of the result. But we all know that certain things would be impossible that are now practiced by church members.

"What would Jesus do about the great army of unemployed and desperate who tramp the streets and curse the Church, or are indifferent to it, lost in the bitter struggle for the bread that tastes bitter when it is earned on account of the desperate conflict to get it?

"What would Jesus do? Is not that what the disciple ought to do? Is he not commanded to follow in His steps? What does the age need more than personal sacrifice? Is it true that the Christian disciples today in most of our churches are living soft, easy, and selfish lives, very far from any sacrifice that can be called sacrifice? What would Jesus do?

"It is the personal element that Christian discipleship needs to emphasize. Each individual Christian businessman, citizen, needs to follow in His steps along the path of personal sacrifice to Him. There is not a different path today from that of Jesus' own times. It is the same path. Nothing but a discipleship of this kind can face the destructive selfishness of the age with any hope of overcoming it.

"There is a great quantity of nominal Christianity today. There is need of more of the real kind. We need revival of the Christianity of Christ. We have unconsciously, lazily, selfishly, formally grown into a discipleship that Jesus Himself would not acknowledge. Is it possible for this church to sing with exact truth, 'Jesus, I my cross have taken, all to leave and follow Thee'? If we can sing that truly, then we may claim discipleship. But if our definition of being a Christian is simply to enjoy the privileges of worship, be generous at no expense to ourselves, have a good, easy time surrounded by pleasant friends and by comfortable things, live respectably, and at the same time avoid the world's great stress of sin and trouble because it is too much pain to bear it, surely we are a long way from following the steps of Him who trod the way with groans and tears and sobs of anguish for a lost humanity; who sweat, as it were, great drops of blood; who cried out on the cross, 'My God, my God, why hast thou forsaken me?'

"Are we ready to make and live a new discipleship? Are we ready to reconsider our definition of a Christian? What is it to be a Christian? It is to imitate Jesus. It is to do as He would do. It is to walk in His steps."

When Henry Maxwell finished his sermon, he paused and looked at the people with a look they never forgot. A great silence fell over the congregation. Everyone expected the preacher to call for volunteers who would do as Jesus would do. But Maxwell had been led by the Spirit to deliver his message this time and wait for results to come.

He closed the service with a tender prayer that kept the Divine Presence lingering very near every hearer, and the people slowly rose to go out. Then men and women in great numbers crowded around the platform to see Mr. Maxwell and to bring him the promise of their consecration to the pledge to do as Jesus would do. That was a remarkable day in the history of that church, but even more so in the history of Henry Maxwell. He left the meeting very late. He went to his room at the Settlement, and after an hour with the Bishop and Dr. Bruce spent in a joyful rehearsal of the wonderful events of the day, he sat down to think over again by himself all the experience he was having as a Christian disciple.

He knelt to pray, as he always did before going to sleep, and it was while he was on his knees that he had a waking vision of what might be in the world when once the new discipleship had made its way into the conscience and conscientiousness of Christendom. He was fully conscious of being awake, but no less certainly did it seem to him that he saw certain results with great distinctiveness, partly as realities. He saw himself going back to the First Church in Raymond, living there in a simpler, more self-denying fashion than he had yet been willing to live. He saw Rachel Winslow and Virginia Page going on with their work of service at the Rectangle and reaching out loving hands of helpfulness far beyond the limits of Raymond. Rachel he saw married to Rollin Page, both fully consecrated to the Master's use, both following His steps with an eagerness intensified and purified by their love for each other. And Rachel's voice sang on, in slums and dark places of despair and sin, and drew lost souls back to God and heaven once more.

He saw Edward Norman, editor of the *News*, creating a force in journalism that in time came to be recognized as one of the real factors of the nation to mold its principles and actually shape its policy.

He saw Jasper Chase, who had denied his Master, growing into a cold, cynical, formal life, writing novels that were social successes but each one with a sting in it, the reminder of his denial, the bitter remorse that, do what he would, no social success could remove.

He saw Felicia and Stephen Clyde happily married, living a beautiful life together, enthusiastic, joyful in suffering, pouring out their great, strong, fragrant service into the dull, dark, terrible places of the great city, and redeeming souls through the personal touch of their home.

He saw Dr. Bruce and the Bishop going on with the Settlement work. He seemed to see the great blazing motto over the door enlarged, "What would Jesus do?" and by this motto everyone who entered the Settlement walked in the steps of the Master.

And now the vision was troubled. Would the church of Jesus throughout the country follow Jesus? Was the movement begun in Raymond to spend itself in a few churches like Nazareth Avenue and the one where he had preached today, and then die away as a local movement, a stirring on the surface but not to extend deep and far? He thought he saw the church of Jesus in America open its heart to the moving of the Spirit and rise to the sacrifice of its ease and self-satisfaction in the name of Jesus. He thought he saw the motto "What would Jesus do?" inscribed over every church door and written on every church member's heart.

He rose at last with the awe of one who has looked at heavenly things and with a hope that walks hand in hand with faith and love.

Steps to Peace With God

1. God's Purpose: Peace and Life

God loves you and wants you to experience peace and life—abundant and eternal.

The Bible Says ...

"We have peace with God through our Lord Jesus Christ." *Romans 5:1, NIV*

"For God so loved the world that He gave His only begotten Son, that whoever believes in Him should not perish but have everlasting life." *John 3:16, NKJV*

"I have come that they may have life, and that they may have it more abundantly." *John 10:10, NKJV*

Since God planned for us to have peace and the abundant life right now, why are most people not having this experience?

2. Our Problem: Separation From God

God created us in His own image to have an abundant life. He did not make us as robots to automatically love and obey Him, but gave us a will and a freedom of choice.

We chose to disobey God and go our own willful way. We still make this choice today. This results in separation from God.

The Bible Says ...

"For all have sinned and fall short of the glory of God." *Romans 3:23, NIV*

"For the wages of sin is death, but the gift of God is eternal life in Christ Jesus our Lord." *Romans 6:23, NIV*

Our choice results in separation from God.

People (Sinful) God (Holy)

OUR ATTEMPTS

Through the ages, individuals have tried in many ways to bridge this gap ... without success ...

THE BIBLE SAYS ...

"There is a way that seems right to a man, but in the end it leads to death."
Proverbs 14:12, NIV

"But your iniquities have separated you from your God; and your sins have hidden His face from you, so that He will not hear."
Isaiah 59:2, NKJV

There is only one remedy for this problem of separation.

3. GOD'S REMEDY: THE CROSS

Jesus Christ is the only answer to this problem. He died on the cross and rose from the grave, paying the penalty for our sin and bridging the gap between God and people.

THE BIBLE SAYS ...

"For there is one God and one mediator between God and men, the man Christ Jesus."
1 Timothy 2:5, NIV

"For Christ also suffered once for sins, the just for the unjust, that He might bring us to God."
1 Peter 3:18, NKJV

"But God demonstrates His own love toward us, in that while we were still sinners, Christ died for us." *Romans 5:8, NKJV*

God has provided the only way ... we must make the choice ...

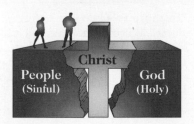

4. Our Response: Receive Christ

We must trust Jesus Christ and receive Him by personal invitation.

The Bible Says ...

"Behold, I stand at the door and knock. If anyone hears My voice and opens the door, I will come in to him and dine with him, and he with Me." *Revelation 3:20, NKJV*

"But as many as received Him, to them He gave the right to become children of God, to those who believe in His name." *John 1:12, NKJV*

"If you confess with your mouth the Lord Jesus and believe in your heart that God has raised Him from the dead, you will be saved." *Romans 10:9, NKJV*

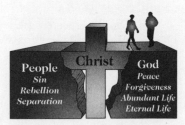

Are you here ... or here?

People
Sin
Rebellion
Separation

Christ

God
Peace
Forgiveness
Abundant Life
Eternal Life

Is there any good reason why you cannot receive Jesus Christ right now?

How to Receive Christ:

1. Admit your need (say, "I am a sinner").
2. Be willing to turn from your sins (repent) and ask for God's forgiveness.
3. Believe that Jesus Christ died for you on the cross and rose from the grave.
4. Through prayer, invite Jesus Christ to come in and control your life through the Holy Spirit (receive Jesus as Lord and Savior).

What to Pray:

Dear Lord Jesus,
    I know that I am a sinner, and I ask for Your forgiveness. I believe You died for my sins and rose from the dead. I turn from my sins and invite You to come into my heart and life. I want to trust and follow You as my Lord and Savior.

In Your Name, Amen.

Date   Signature

GOD'S ASSURANCE: HIS WORD

IF YOU PRAYED THIS PRAYER,

THE BIBLE SAYS ...

"For, 'Everyone who calls on the name of the Lord will be saved.'"
Romans 10:13, NIV

Did you sincerely ask Jesus Christ to come into your life? Where is He right now? What has He given you?

"For it is by grace you have been saved, through faith—and this not from yourselves, it is the gift of God—not by works, so that no one can boast."
Ephesians 2:8–9, NIV

THE BIBLE SAYS ...

"He who has the Son has life; he who does not have the Son of God does not have life. These things I have written to you who believe in the name of the Son of God, that you may know that you have eternal life, and that you may continue to believe in the name of the Son of God."
1 John 5:12–13, NKJV

Receiving Christ, we are born into God's family through the supernatural work of the Holy Spirit who indwells every believer. This is called regeneration or the "new birth."

This is just the beginning of a wonderful new life in Christ. To deepen this relationship you should:

1. Read your Bible every day to know Christ better.
2. Talk to God in prayer every day.
3. Tell others about Christ.
4. Worship, fellowship, and serve with other Christians in a church where Christ is preached.
5. As Christ's representative in a needy world, demonstrate your new life by your love and concern for others.

God bless you as you do.

Billy Graham

If you want further help in the decision you have made, write to:
Billy Graham Evangelistic Association
1 Billy Graham Parkway, Charlotte, North Carolina 28201-0001

CHARLOTTE'S NATIVE SON BECAME
GOD'S AMBASSADOR TO THE WORLD.
EXPERIENCE HIS REMARKABLE JOURNEY HERE.

Visit the Billy Graham Library in Charlotte and retrace the amazing story of one of America's most well-known pastors. Explore historical re-creations, multimedia exhibits, galleries of memorabilia, plus exciting updates including Billy Graham's personal collection of books. Tour the Graham family homeplace, browse unique gifts, or relax over lunch in our café. No matter how you spend your time here, you'll discover an experience that is

FREE

The BILLY GRAHAM Library

MON — TO — SAT 9³⁰-5

704-401-3200

BILLYGRAHAMLIBRARY.ORG

TOTALLY INSPIRING.

Reservations required for groups of 15 or more; call 704-401-3270 or e-mail librarytours@bgea.org.
4330 Westmont Drive (just off Billy Graham Parkway), Charlotte, NC 28217